Holly Jolly Christmas

COLORING BOOK FOR ADULTS

By The Theme Party

If you have any feedback about this book, please contact us at hello@thethemeparty.com

Copyright © 2020 by the theme party

All rights reserved. No part of this publication may be reproduced, distributed, or transmitted in any form or by any means, including photocopying, recording, or other electronic or mechanical methods, without the prior written permission of the publisher.

www.thethemeparty.com

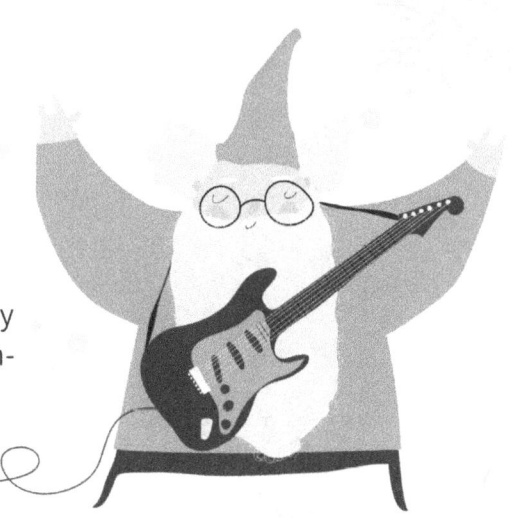

Color Palette Test Page

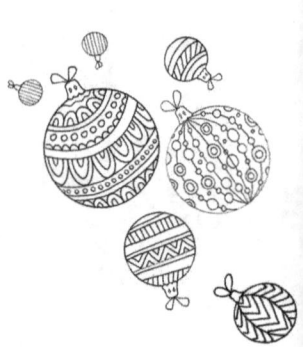

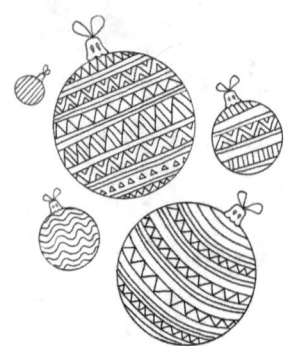

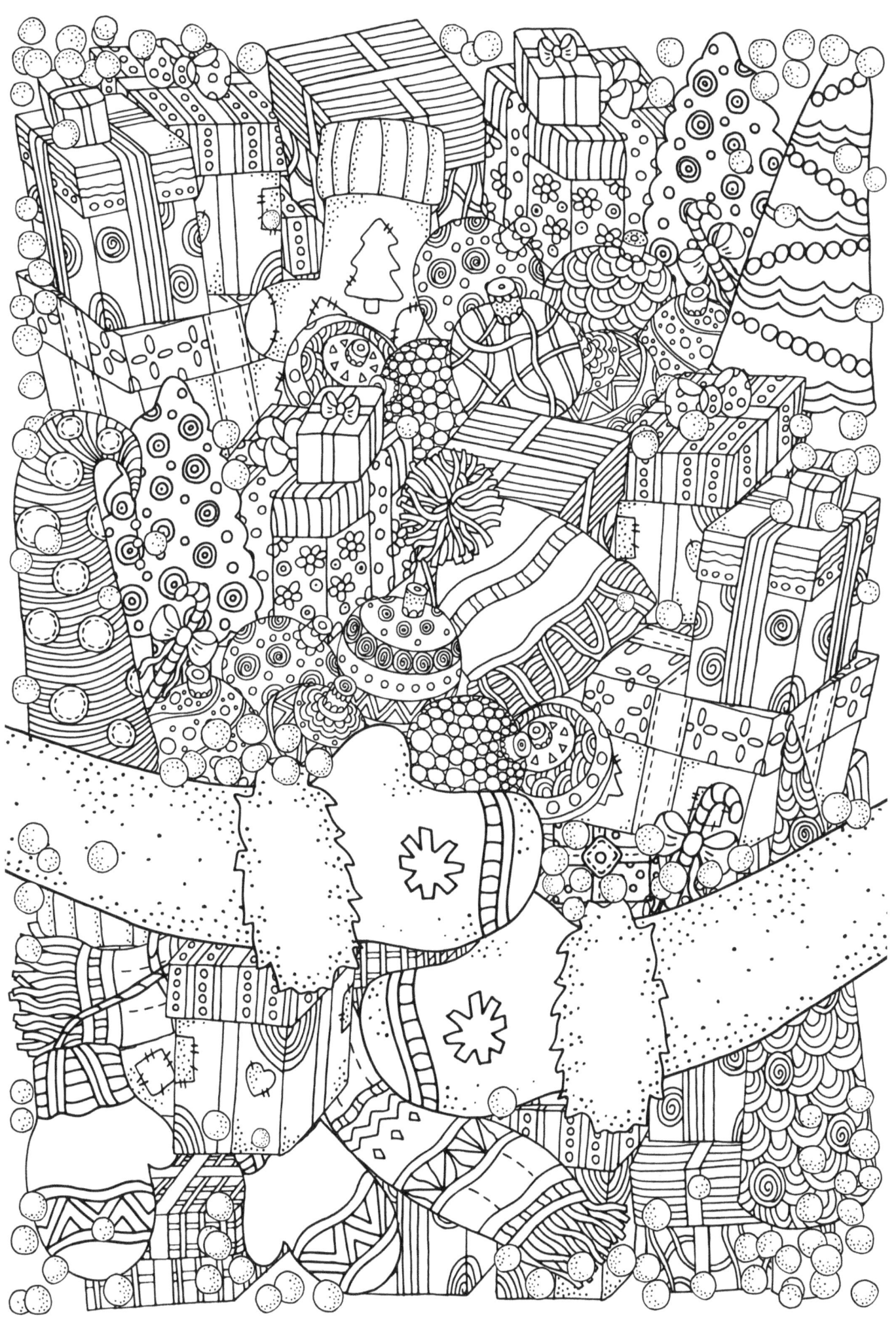

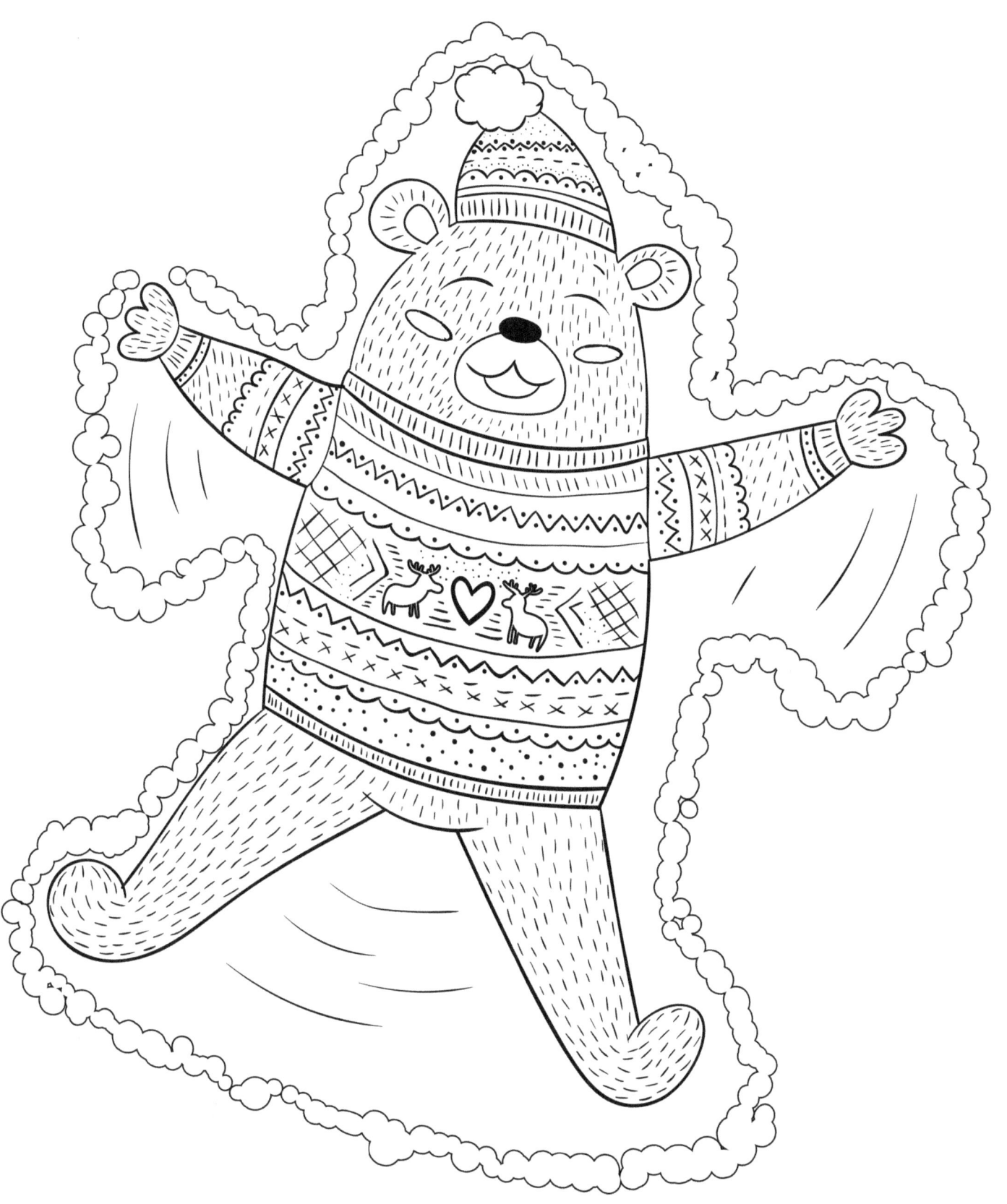

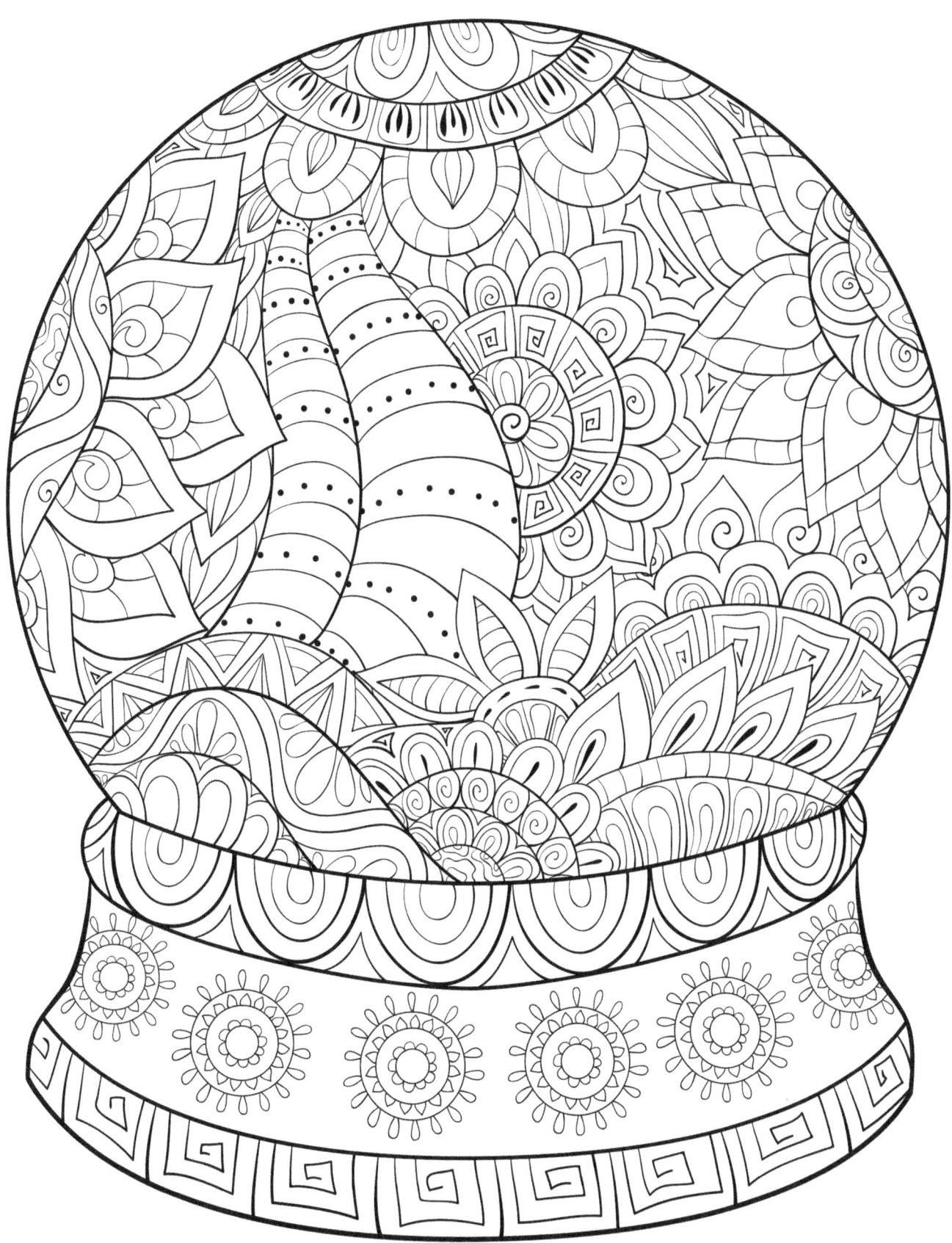

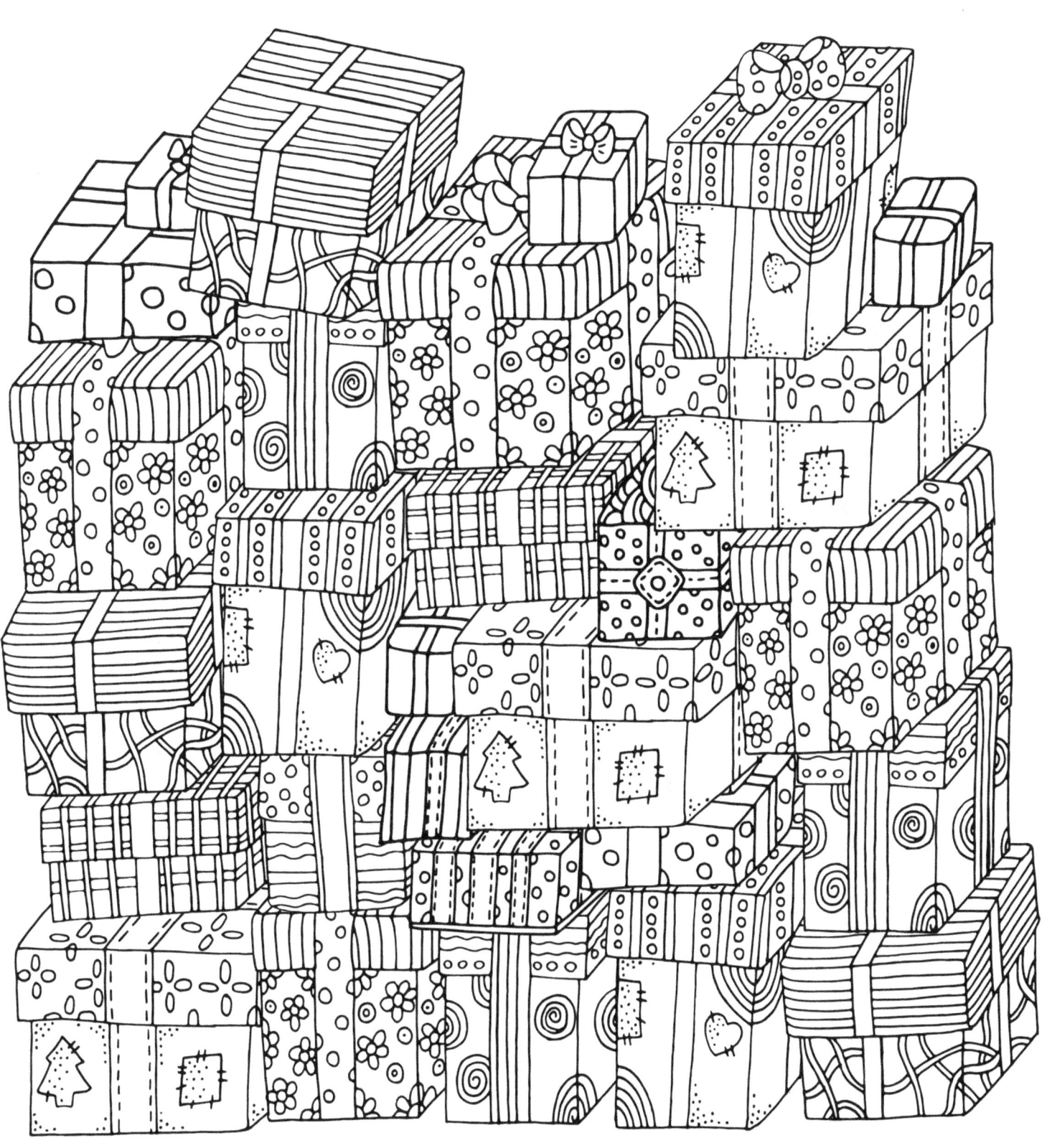

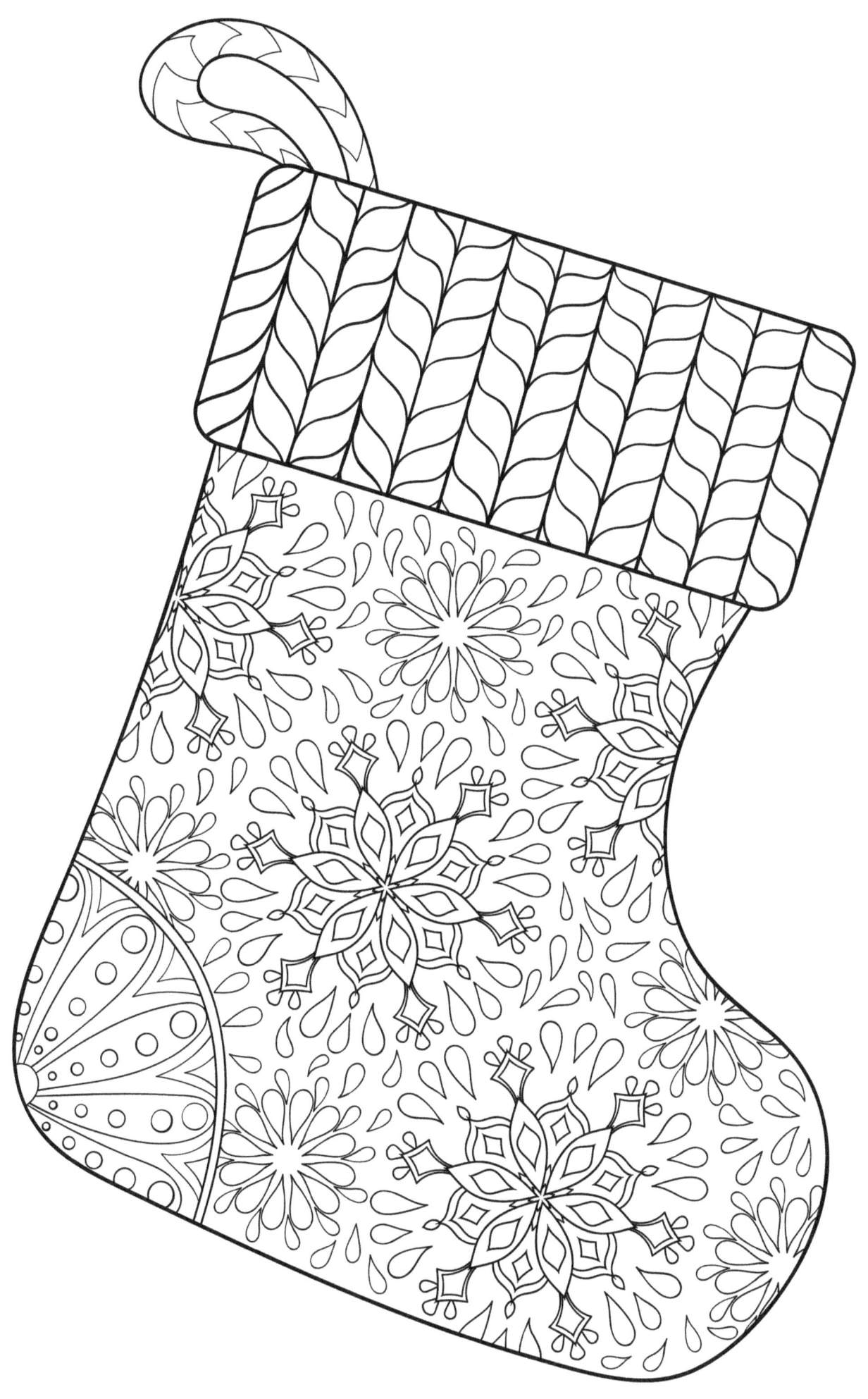

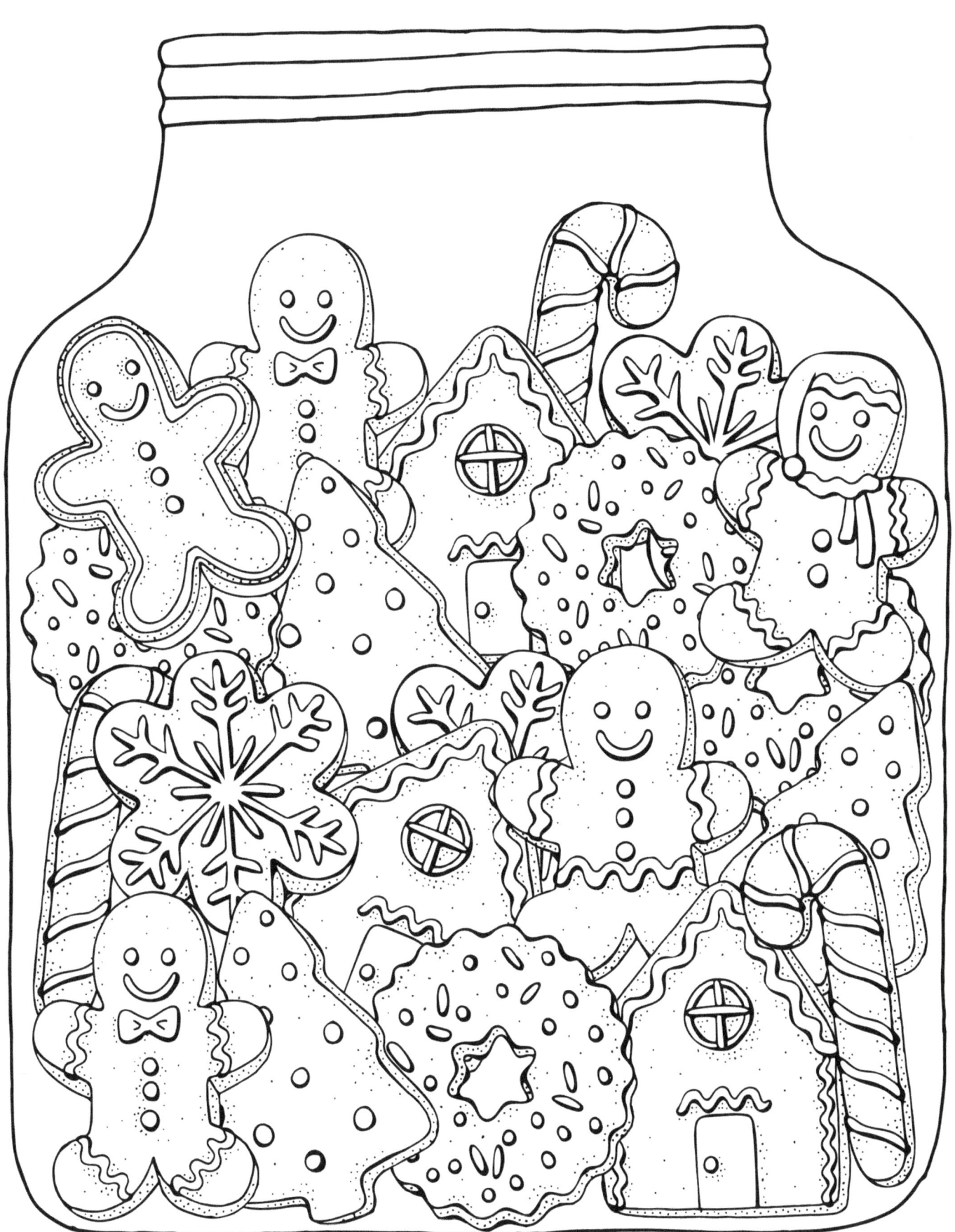

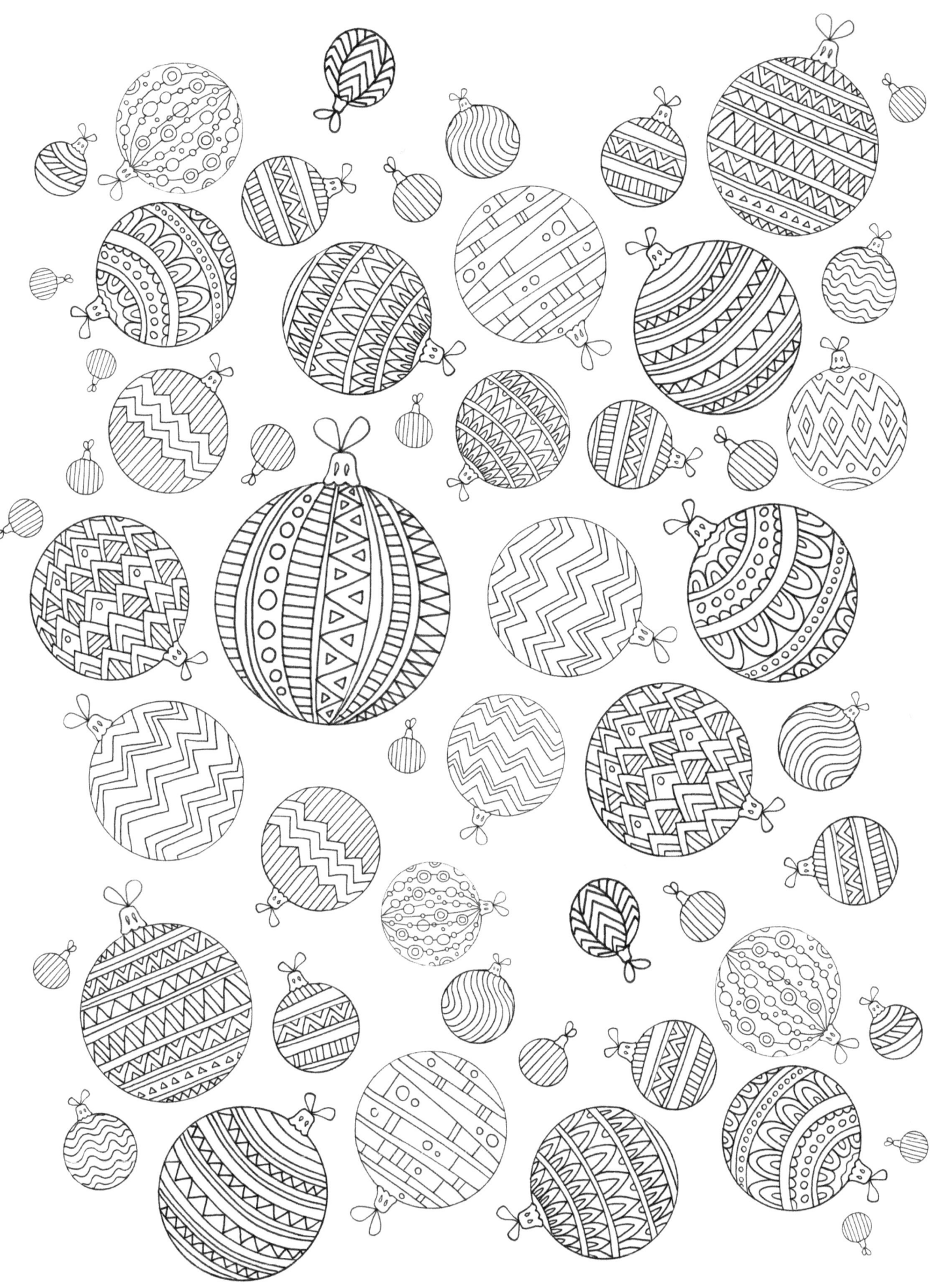

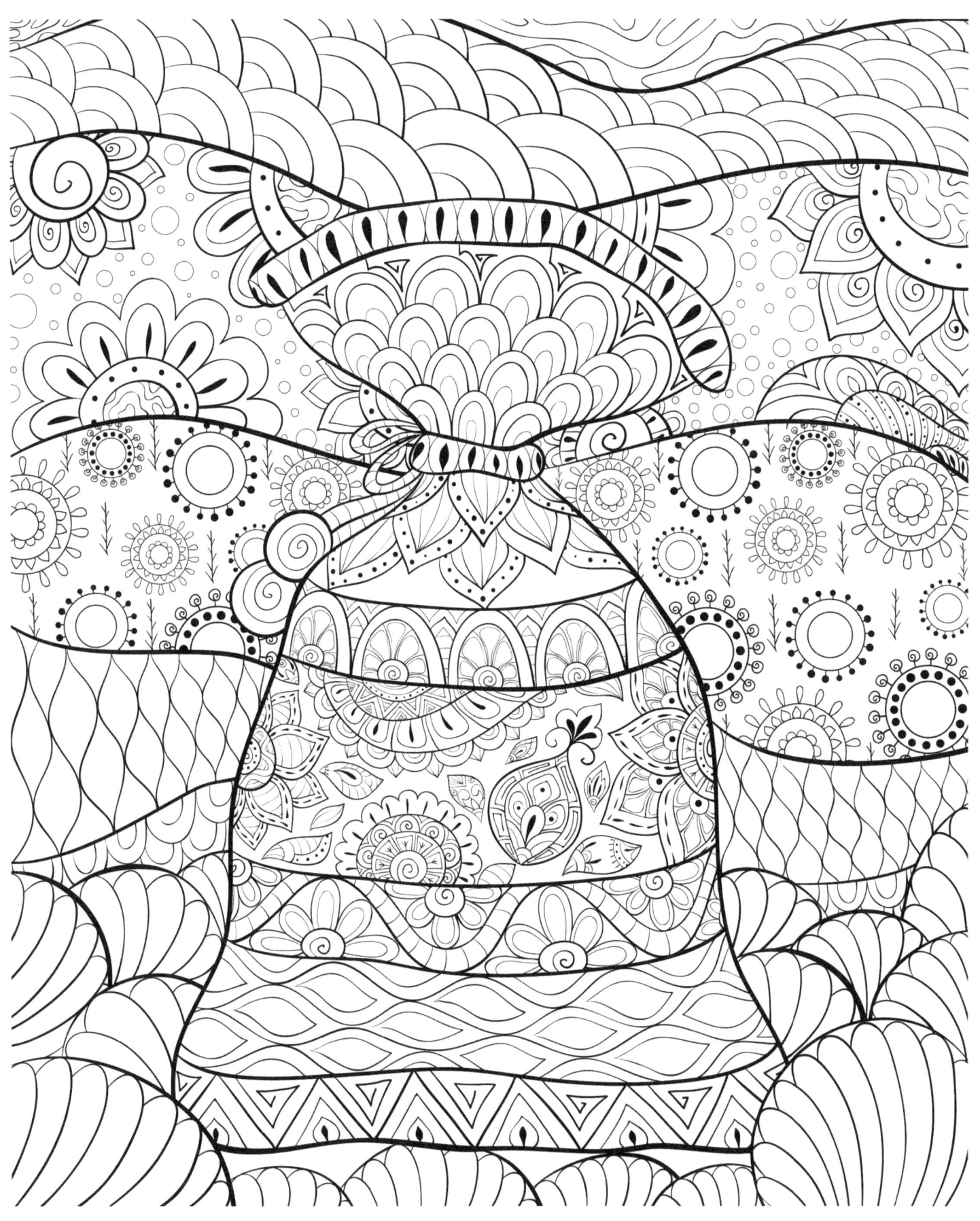

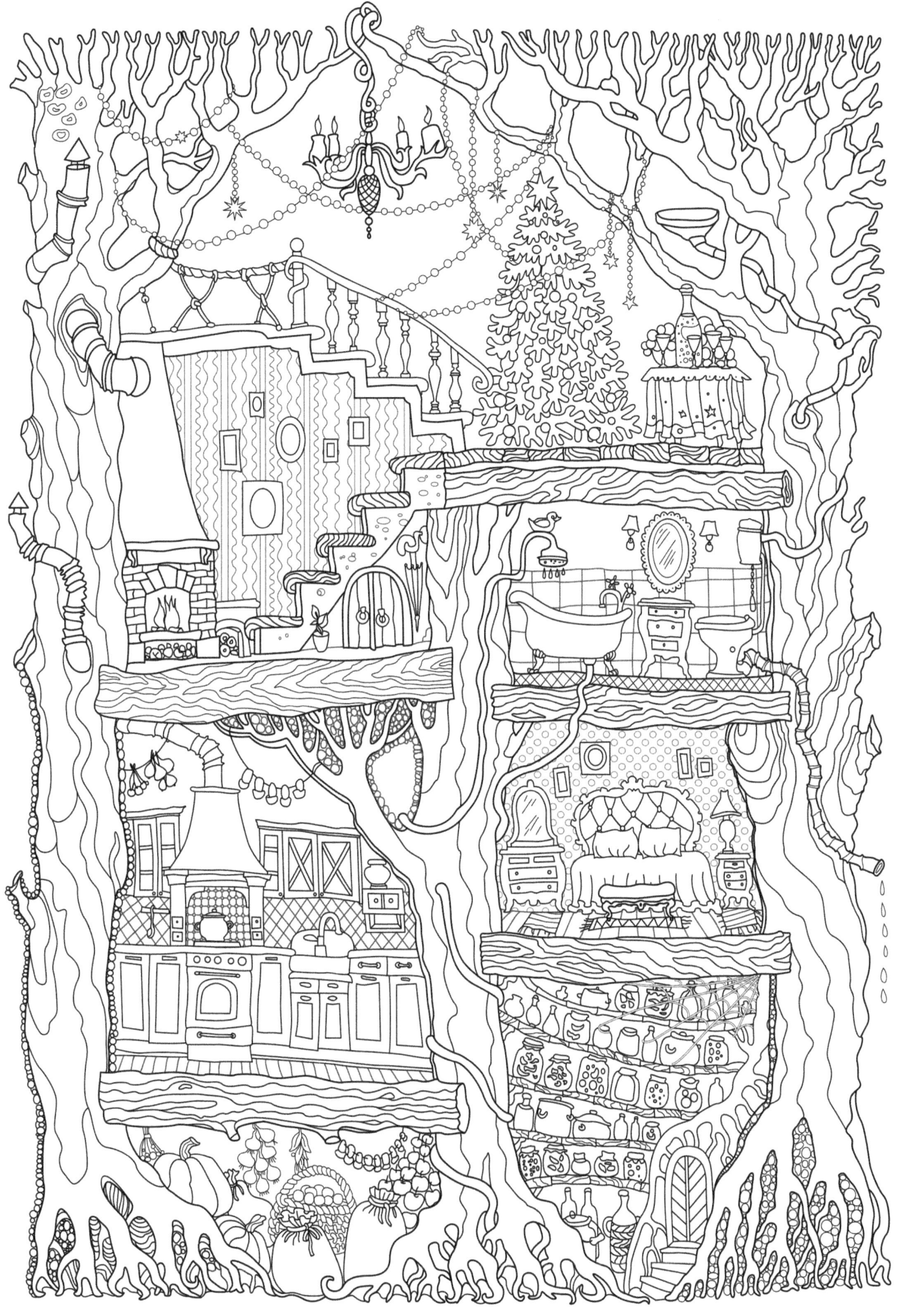

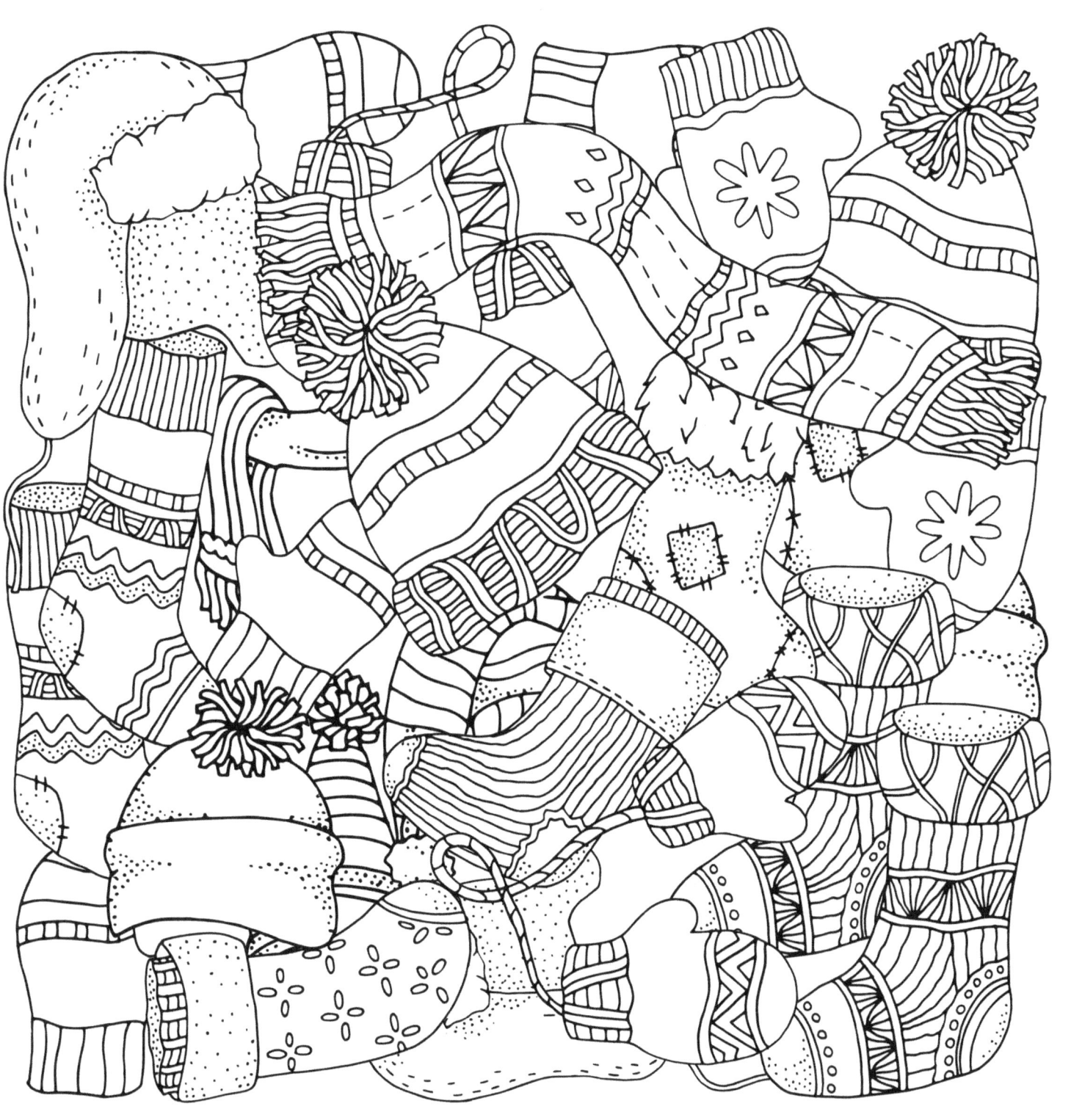

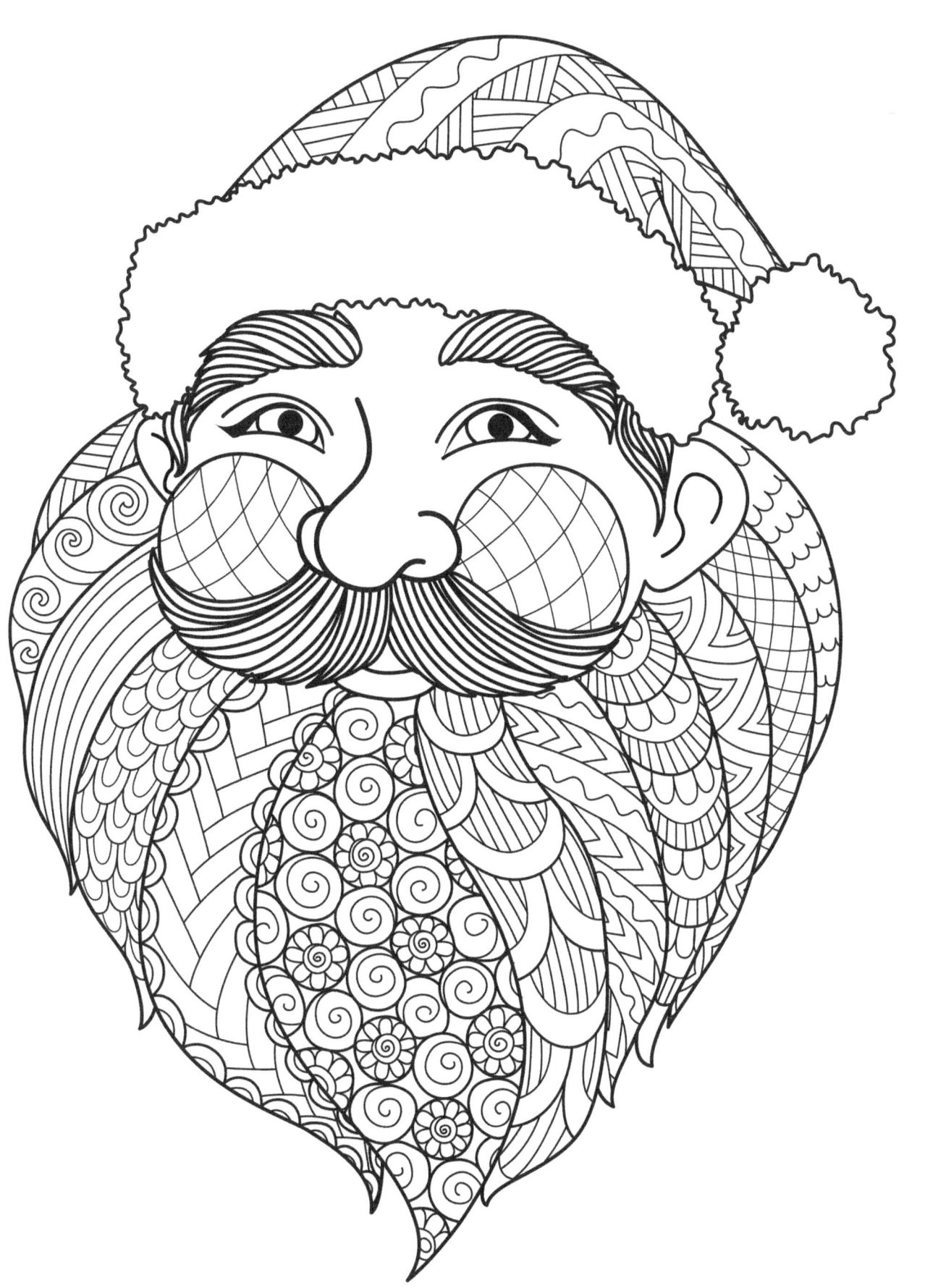

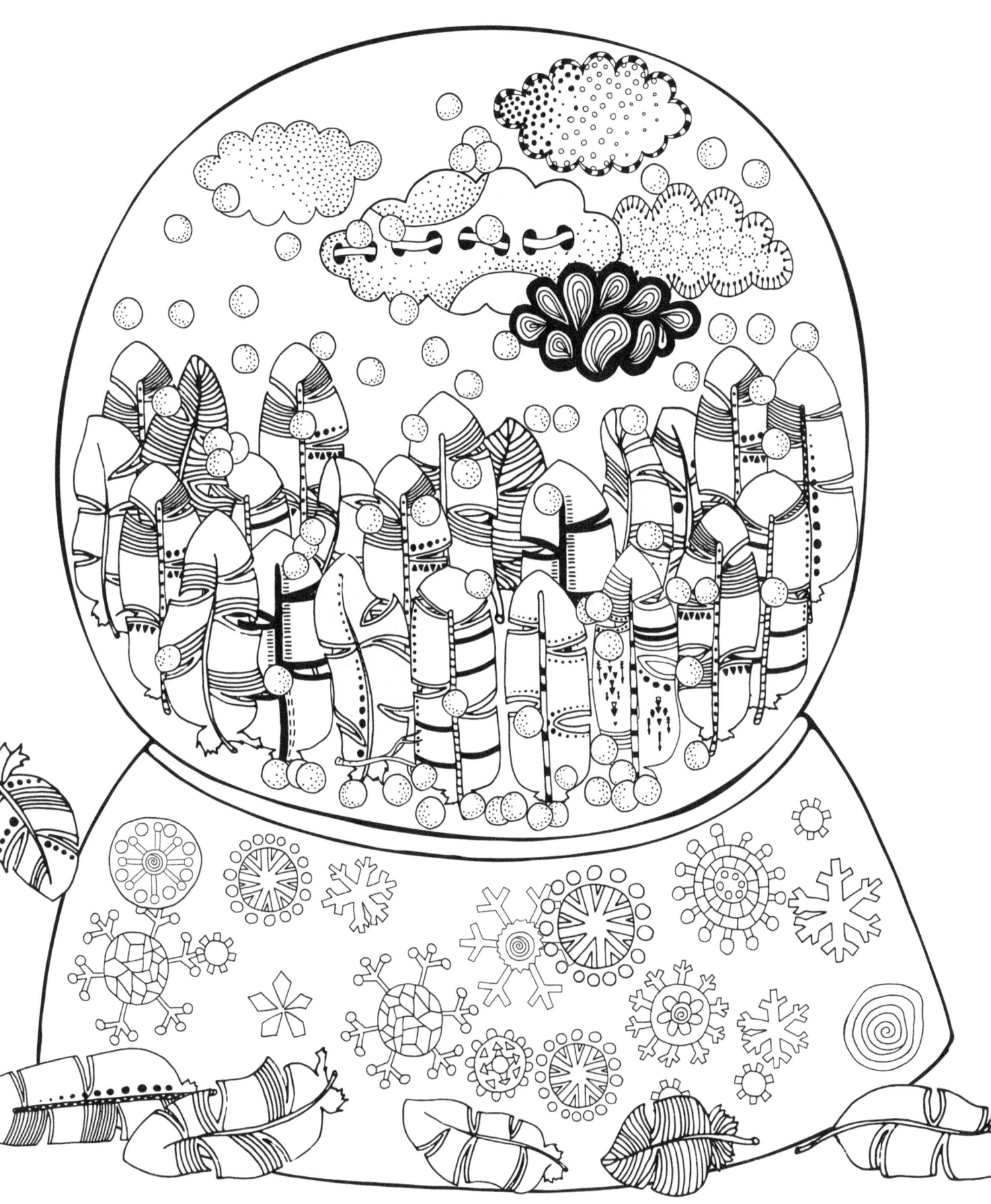

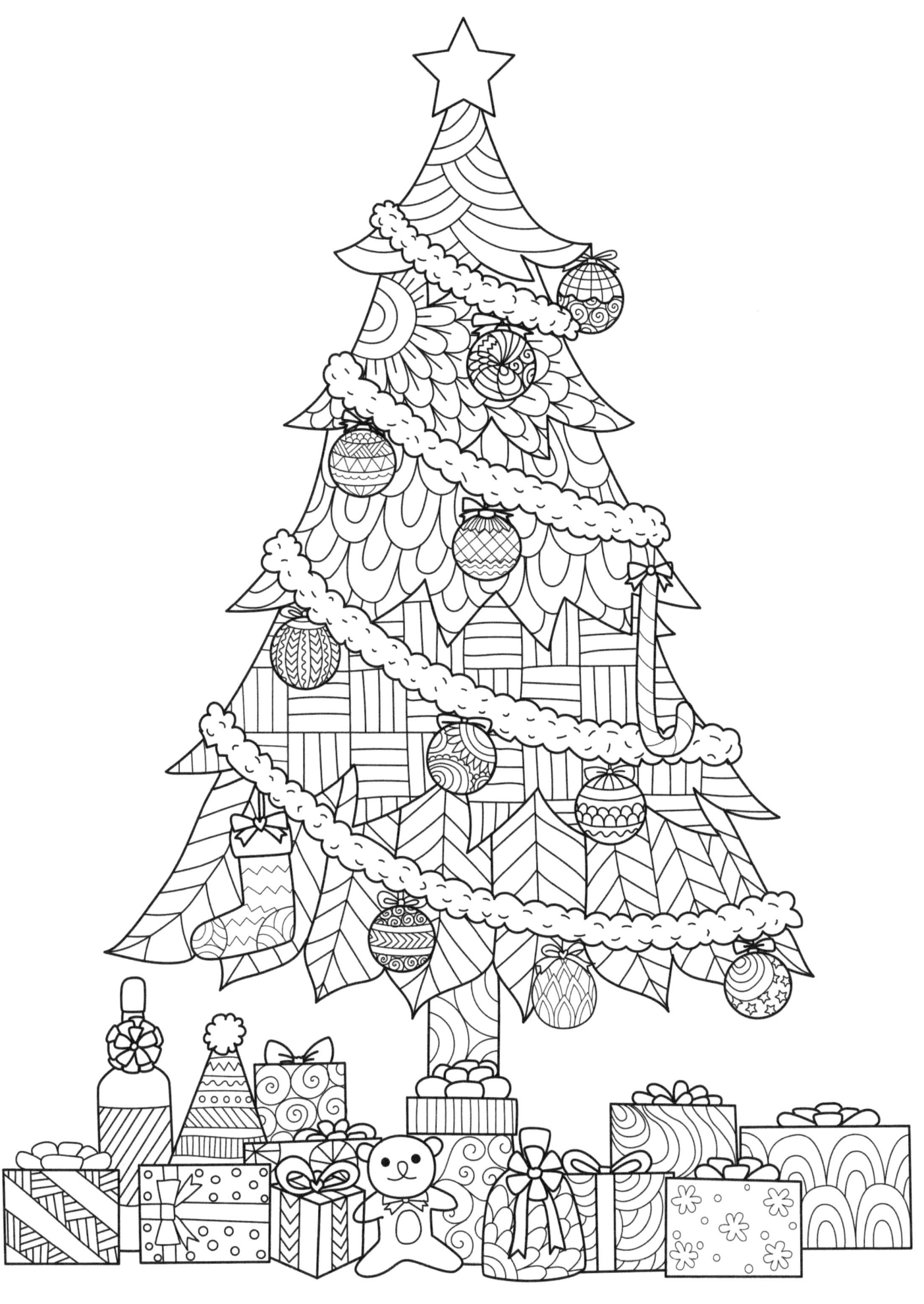

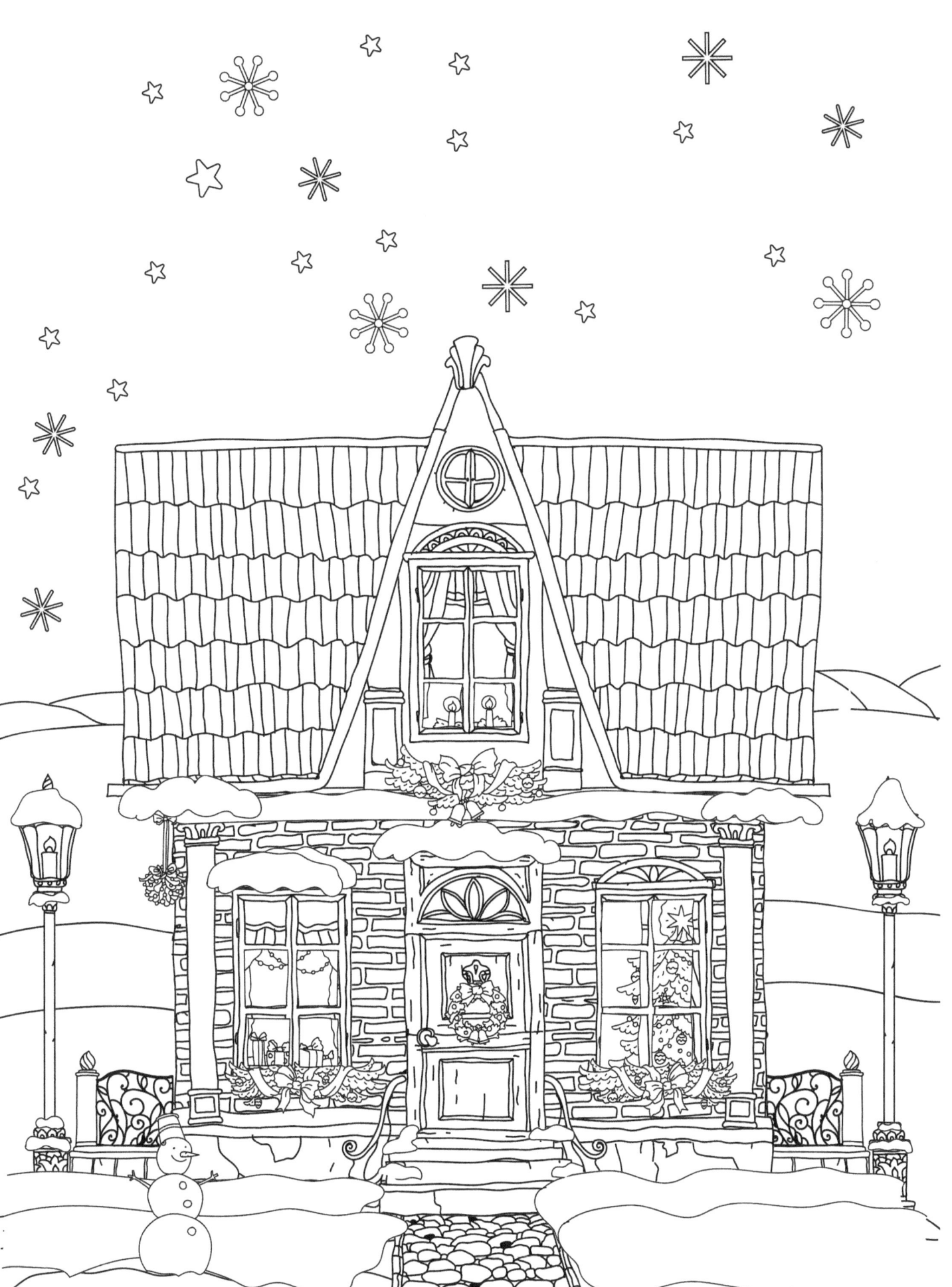

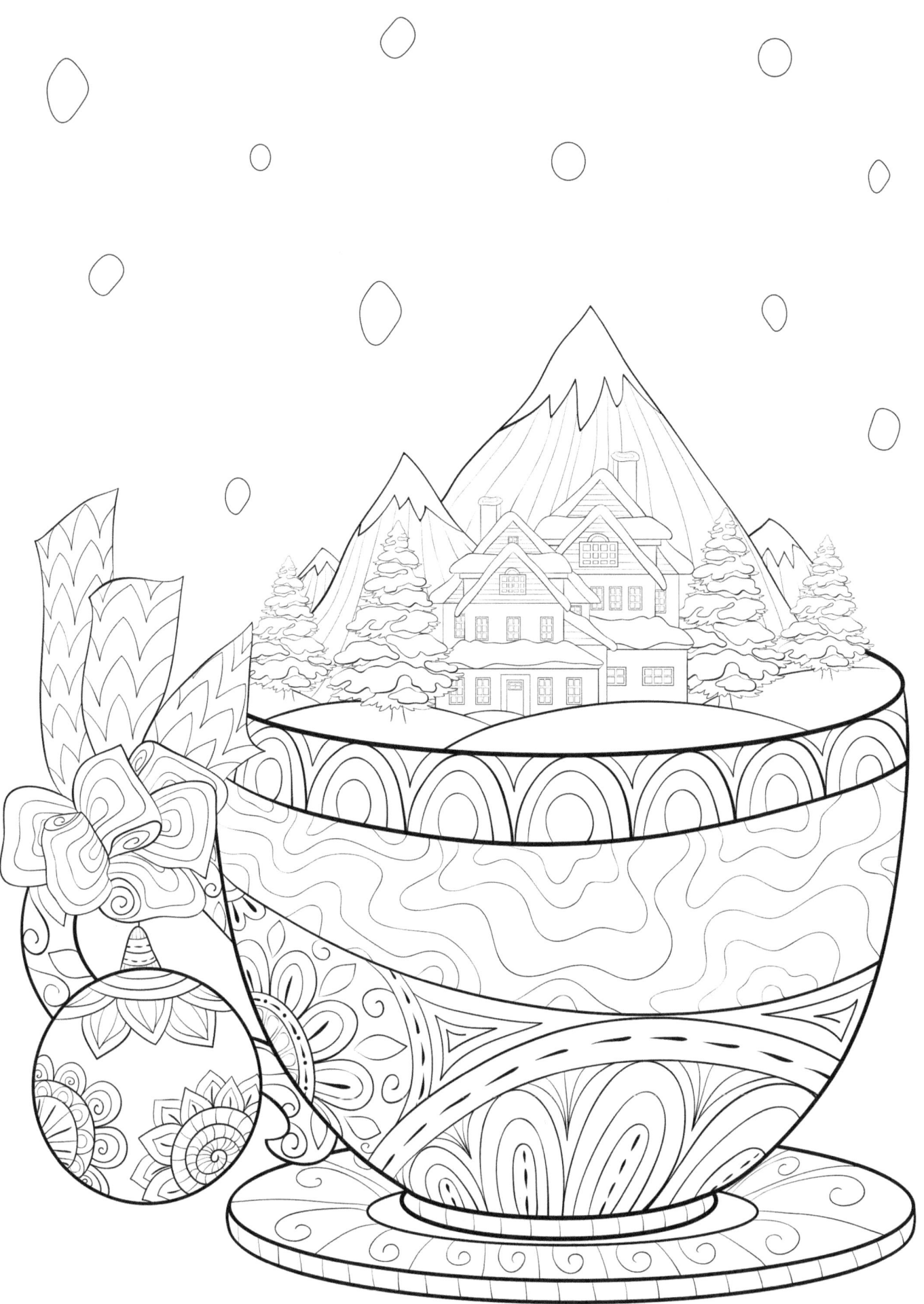

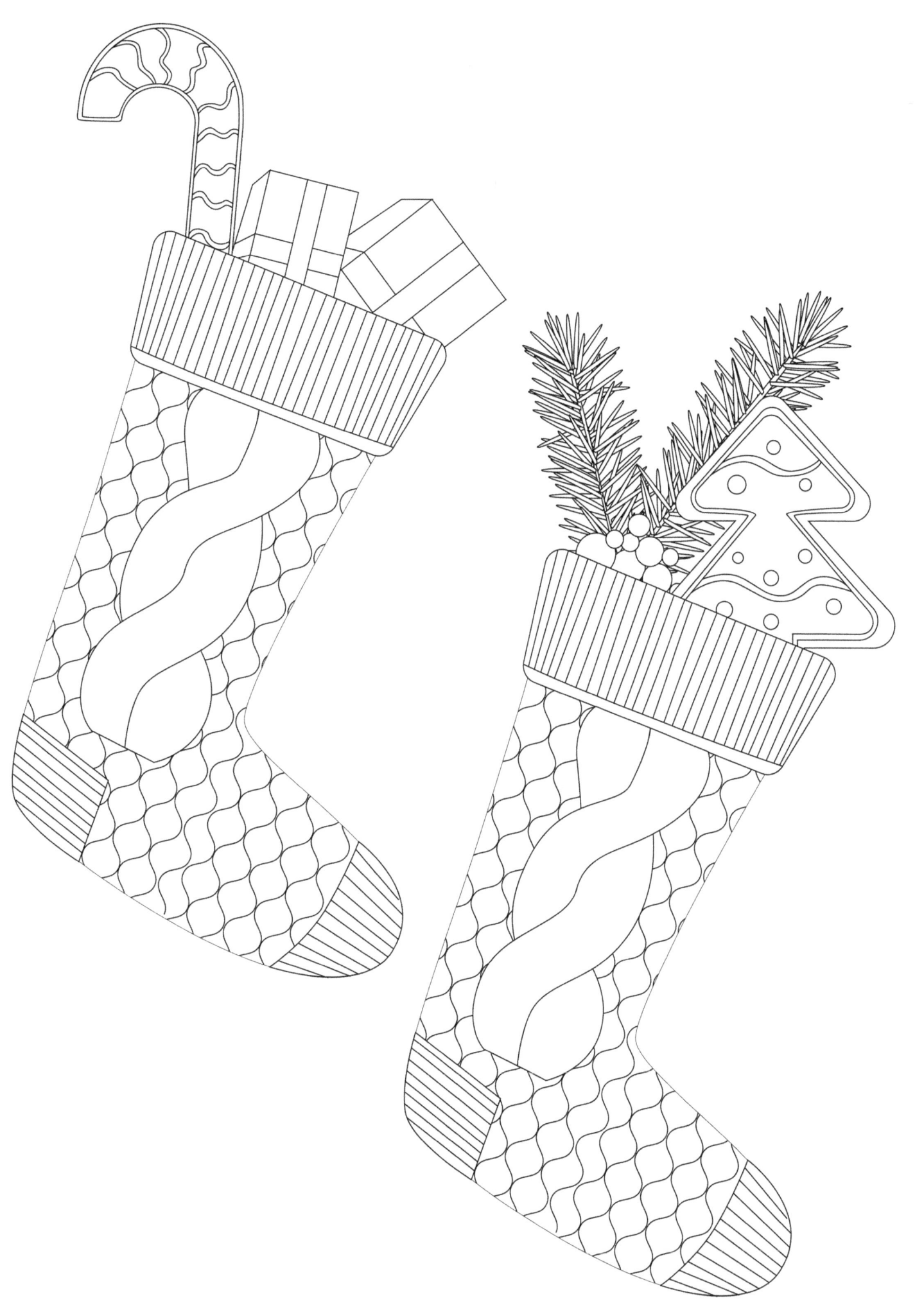

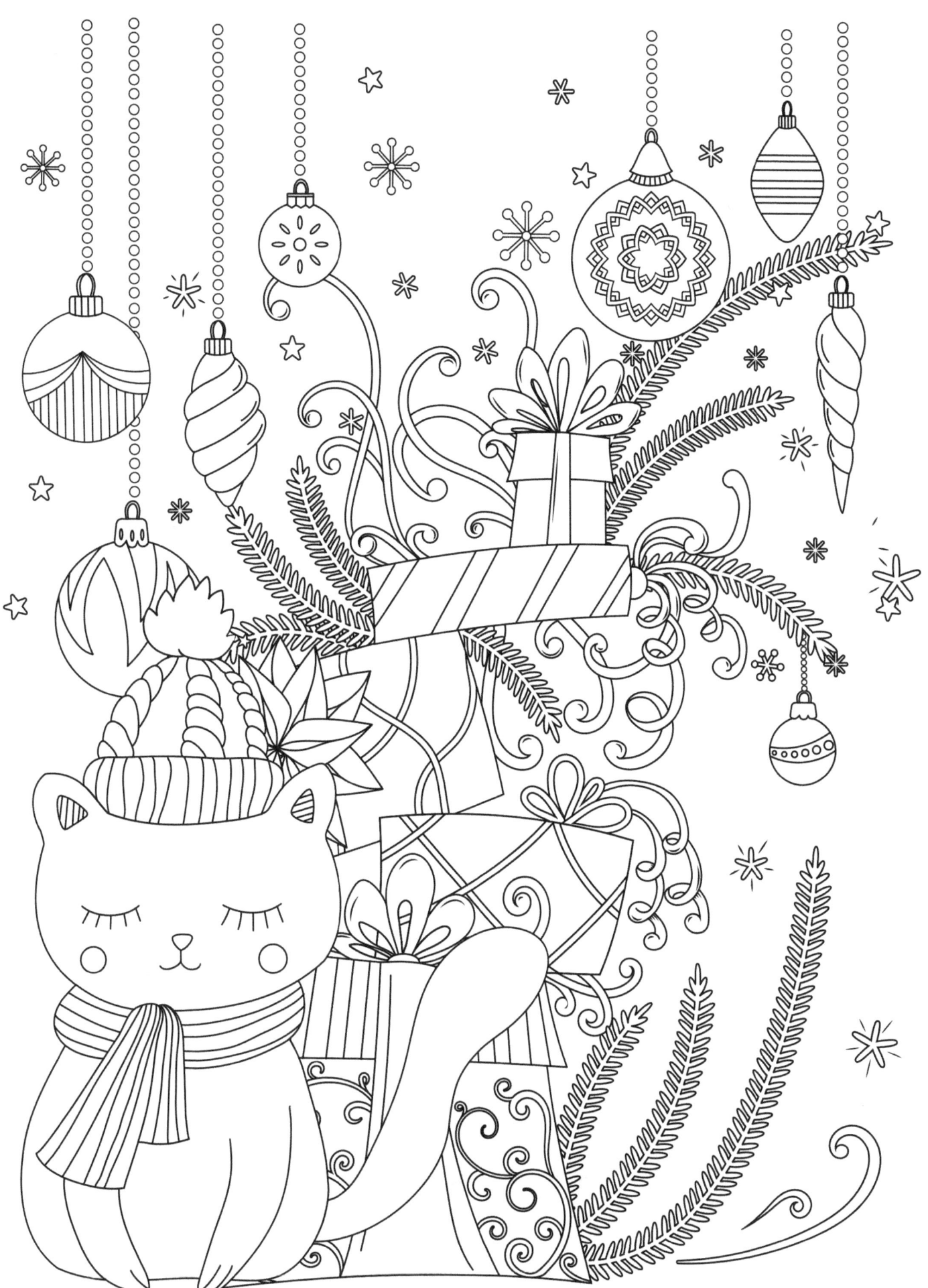

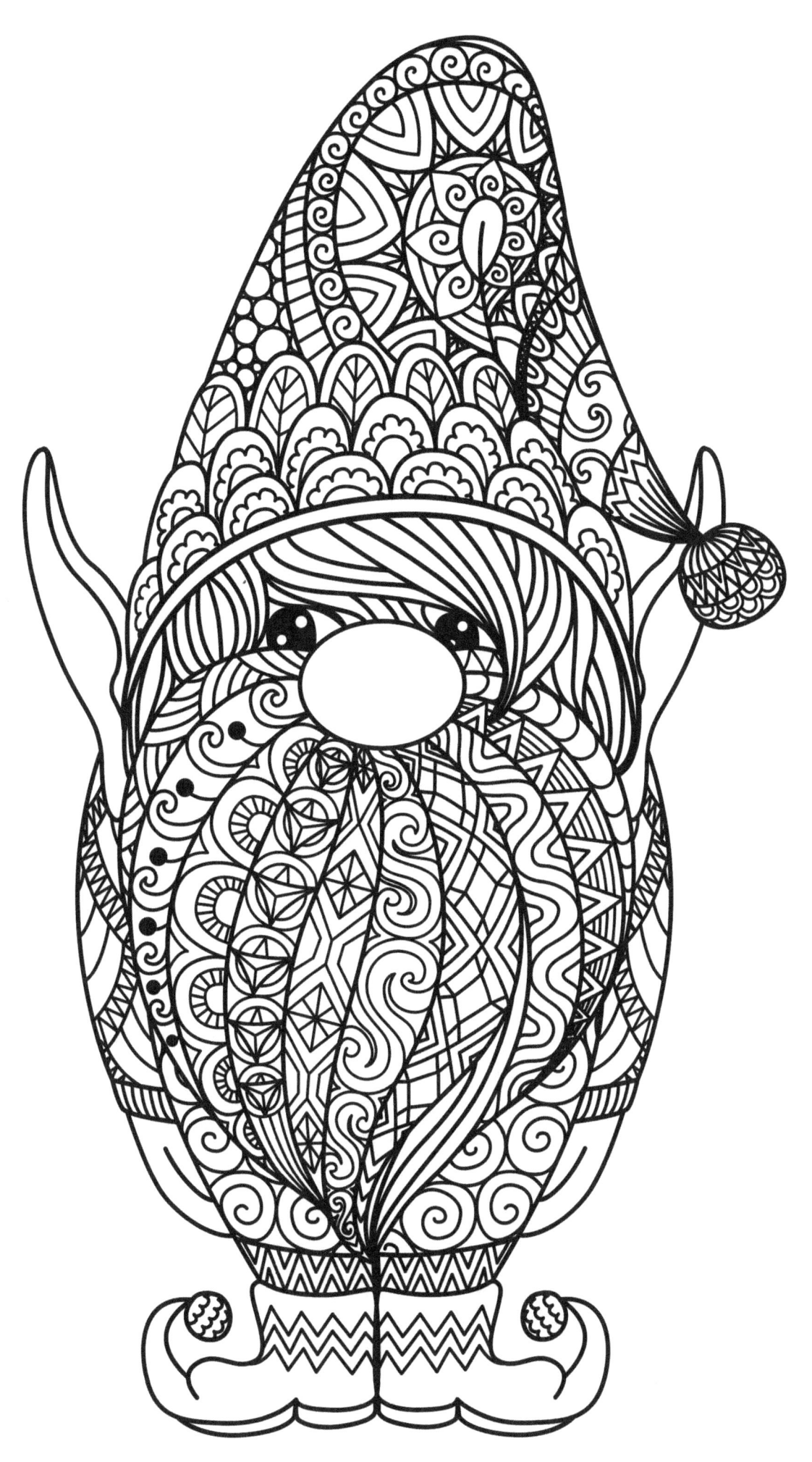

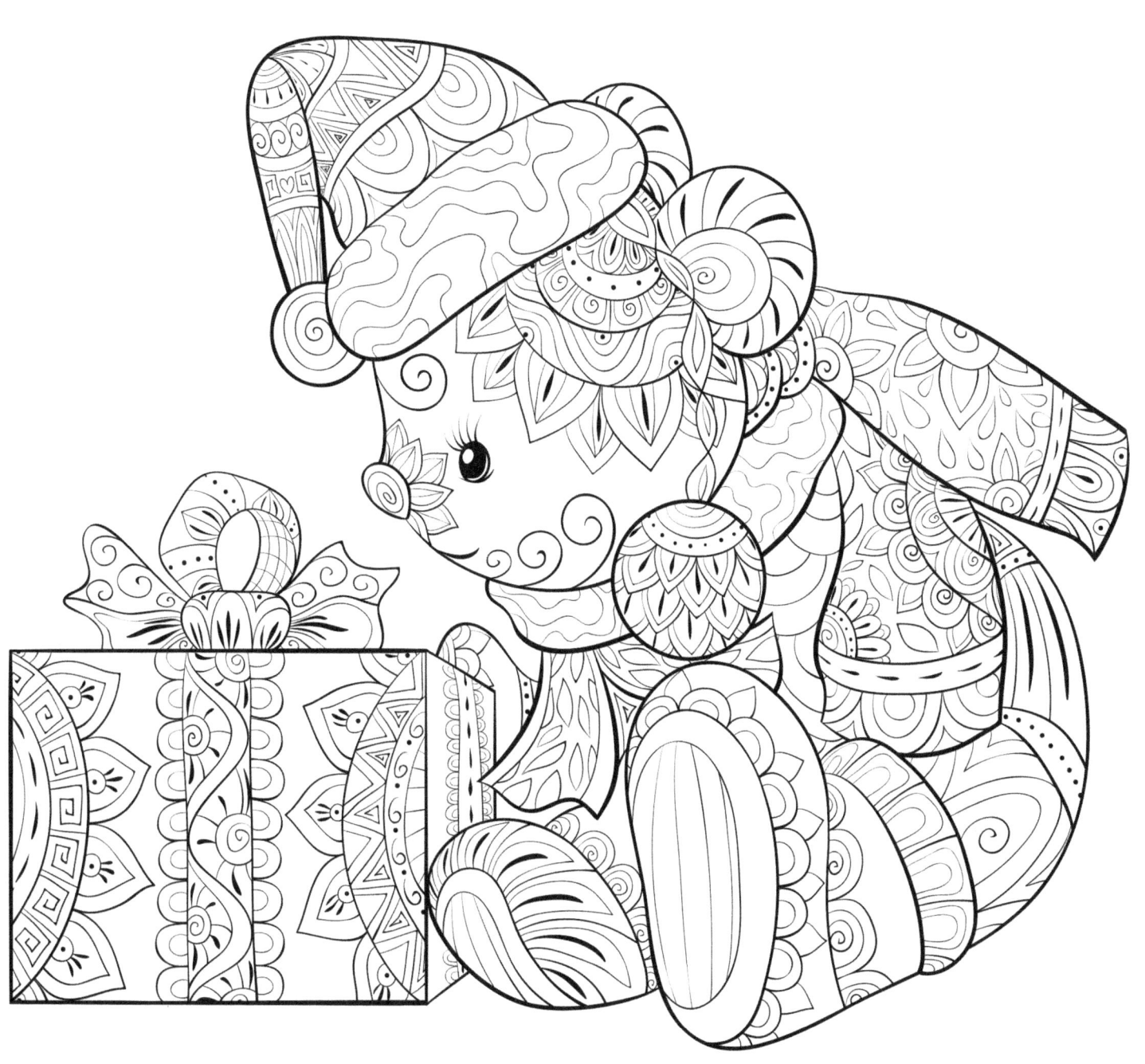

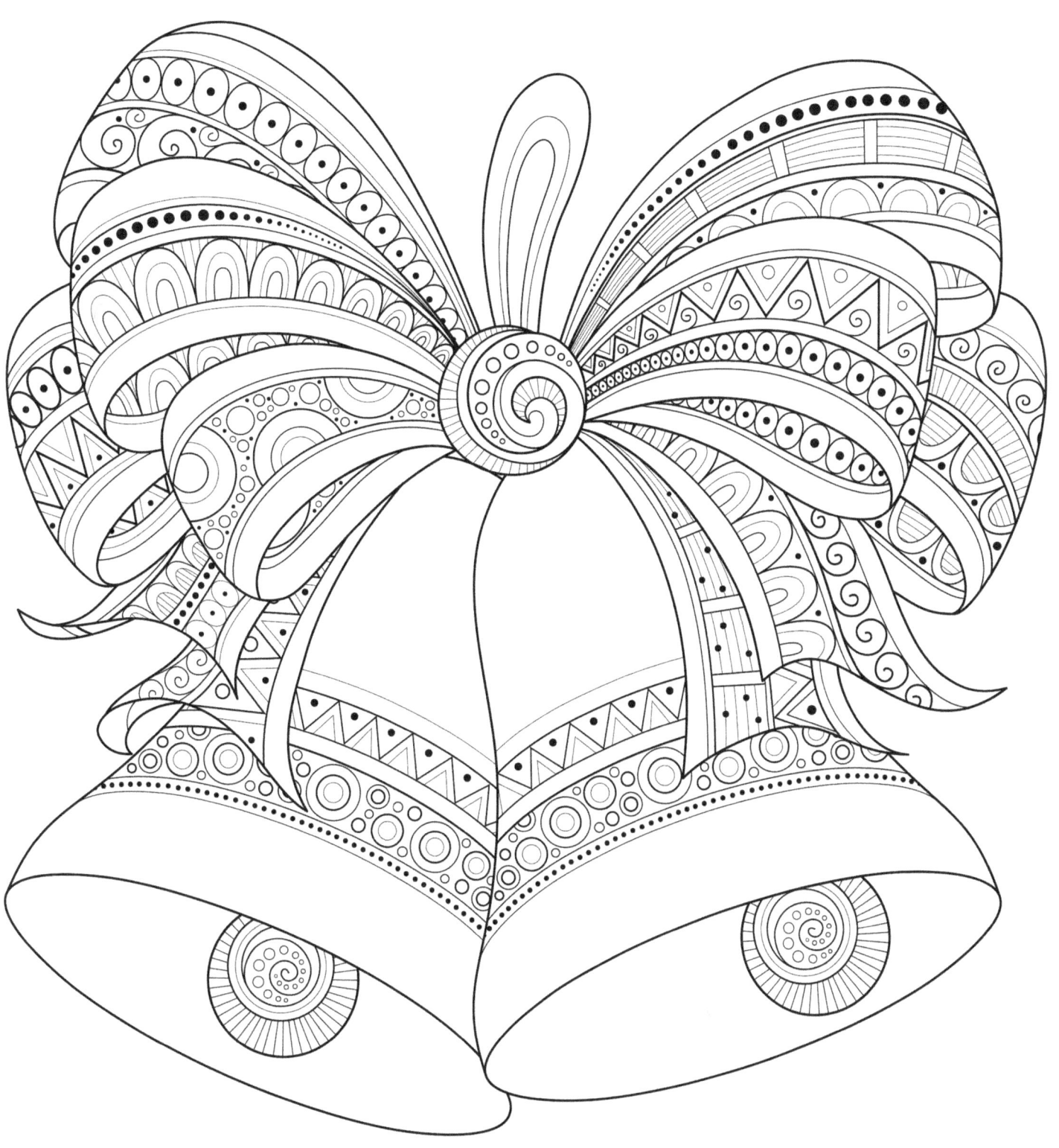

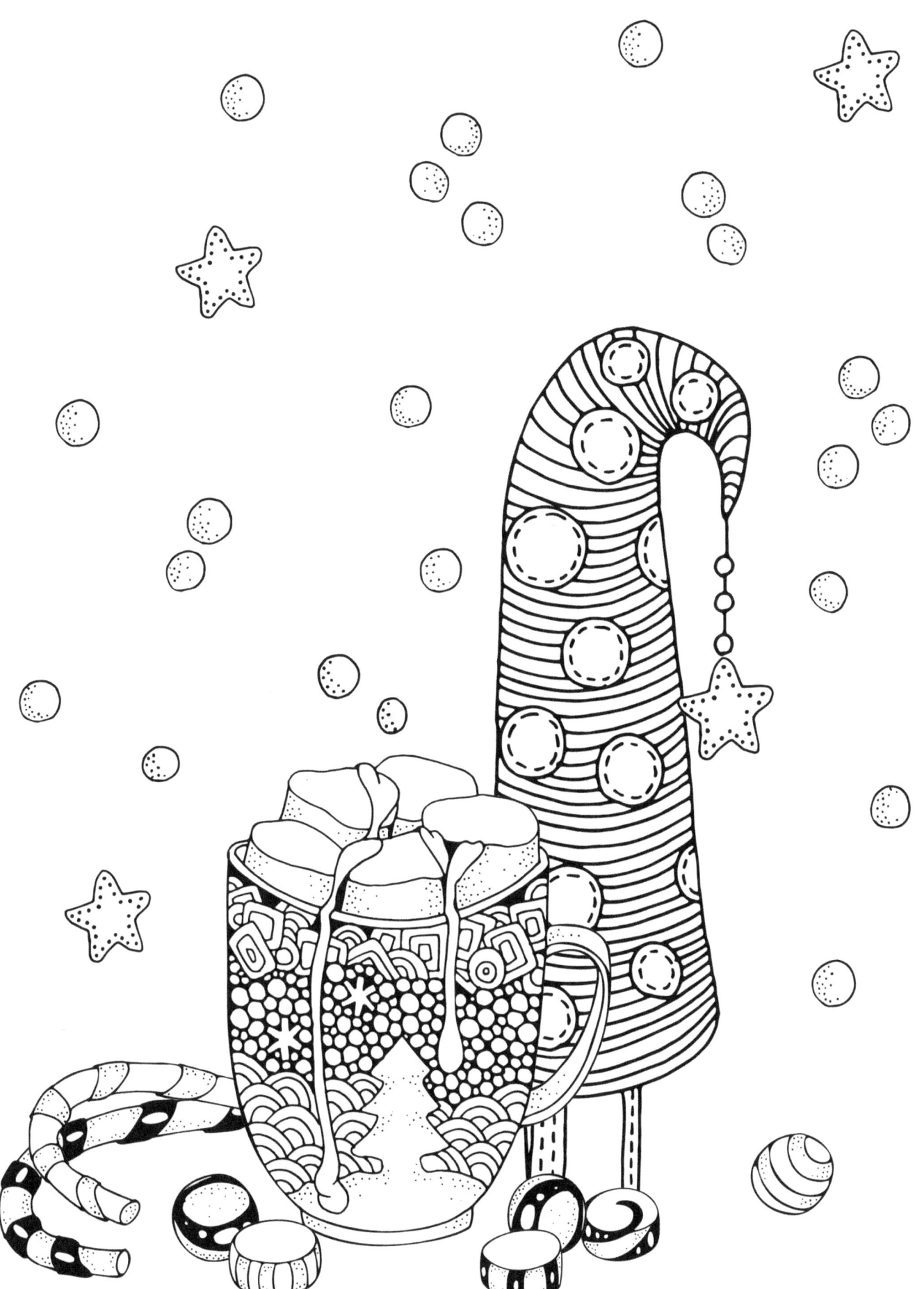

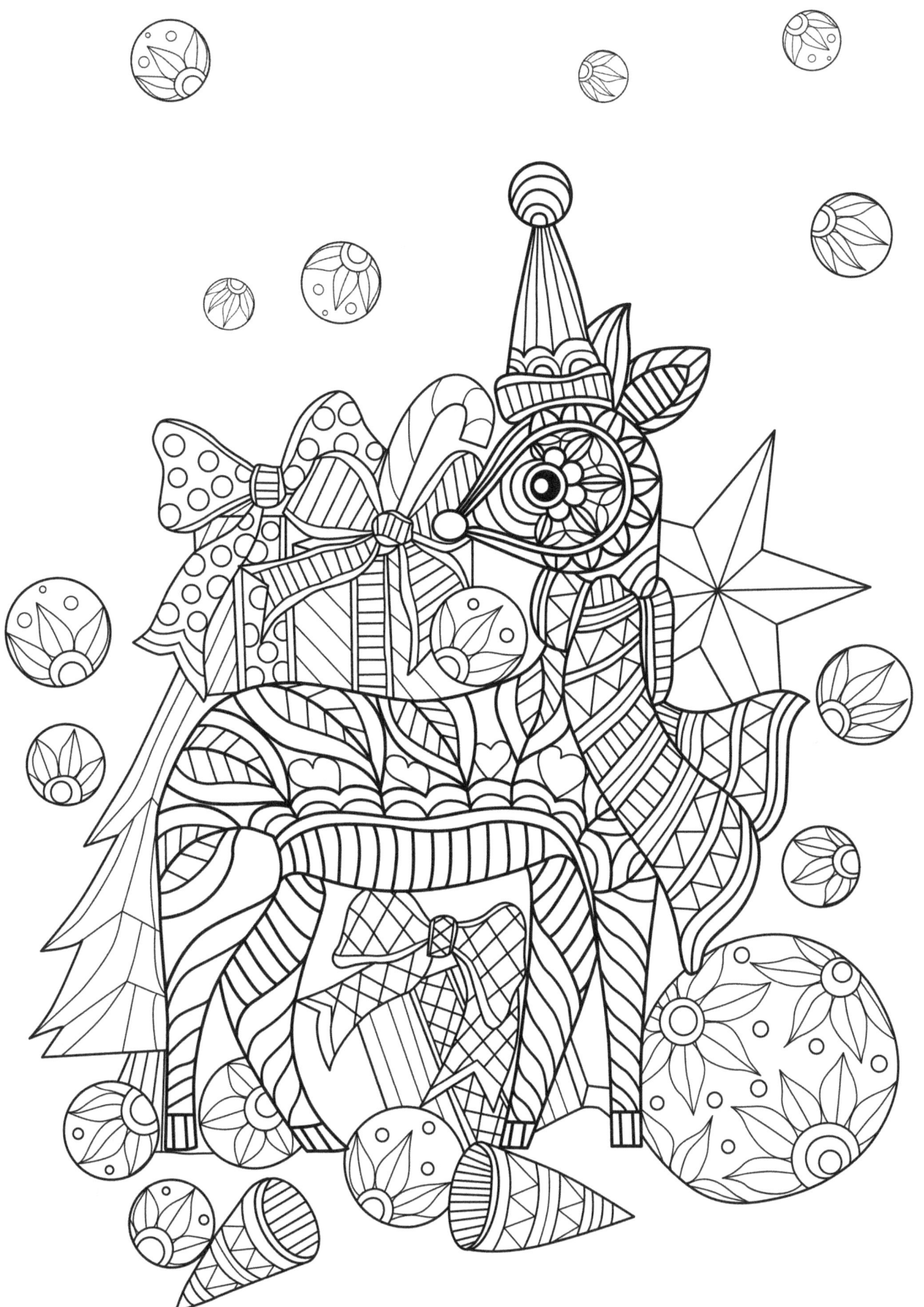

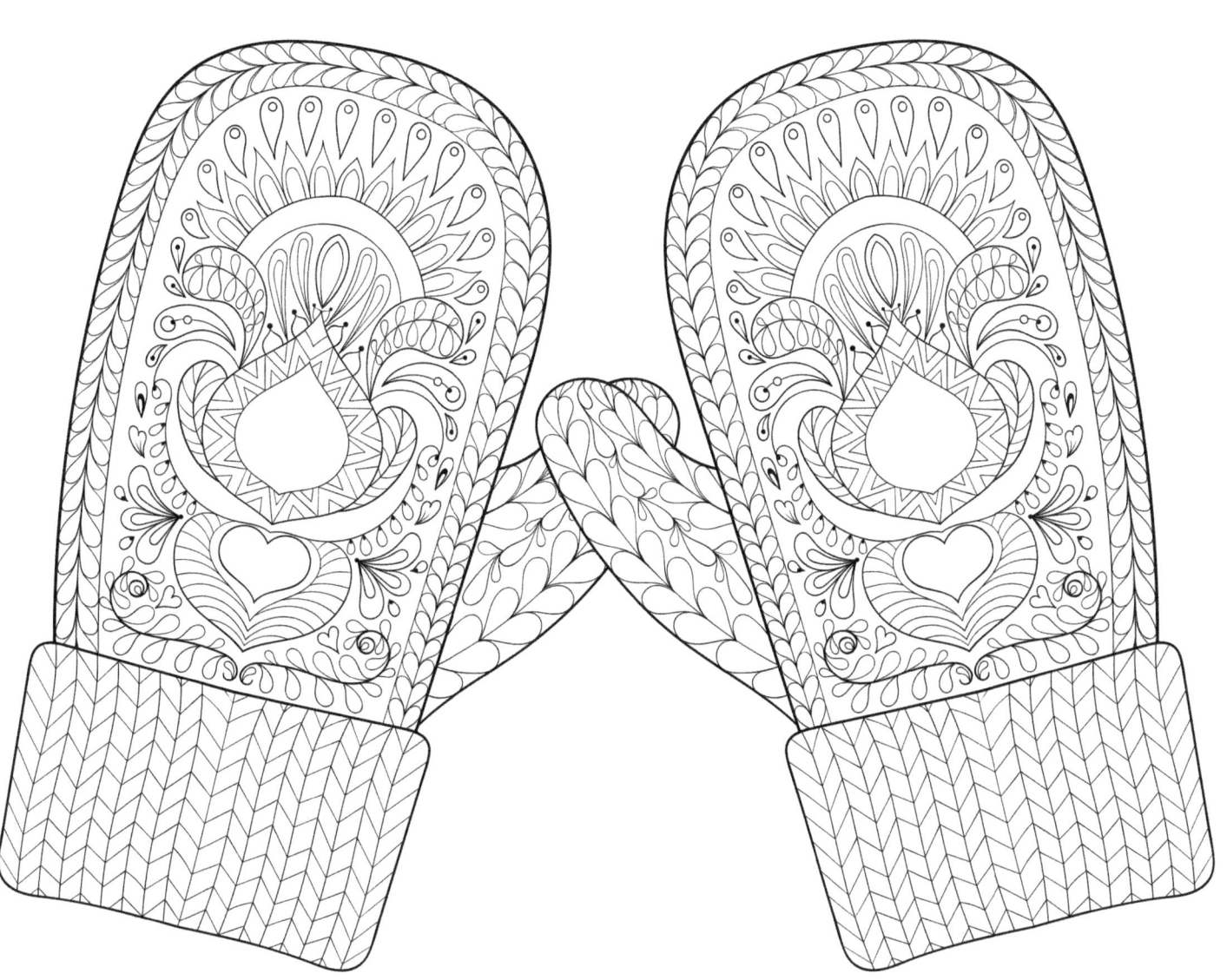

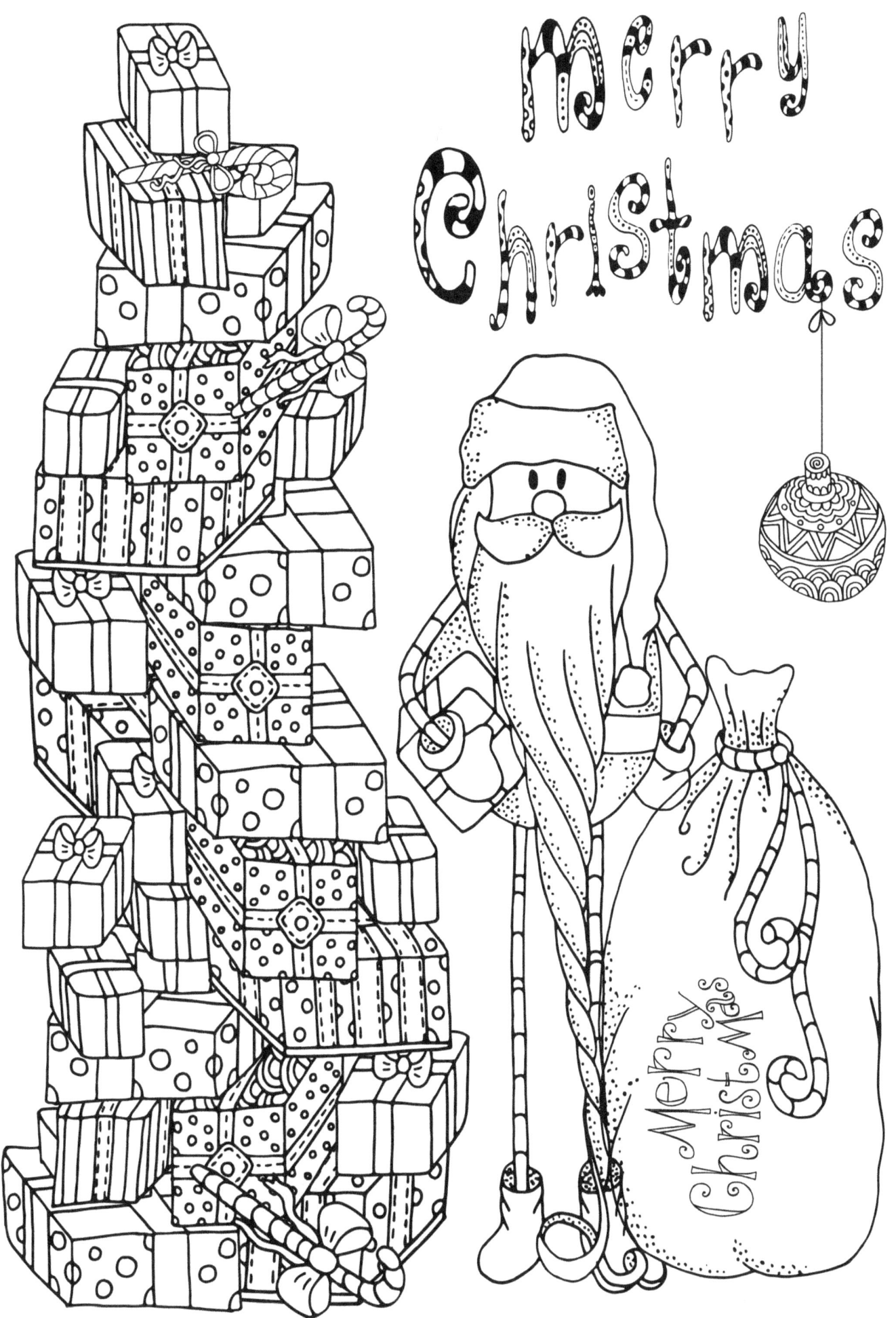

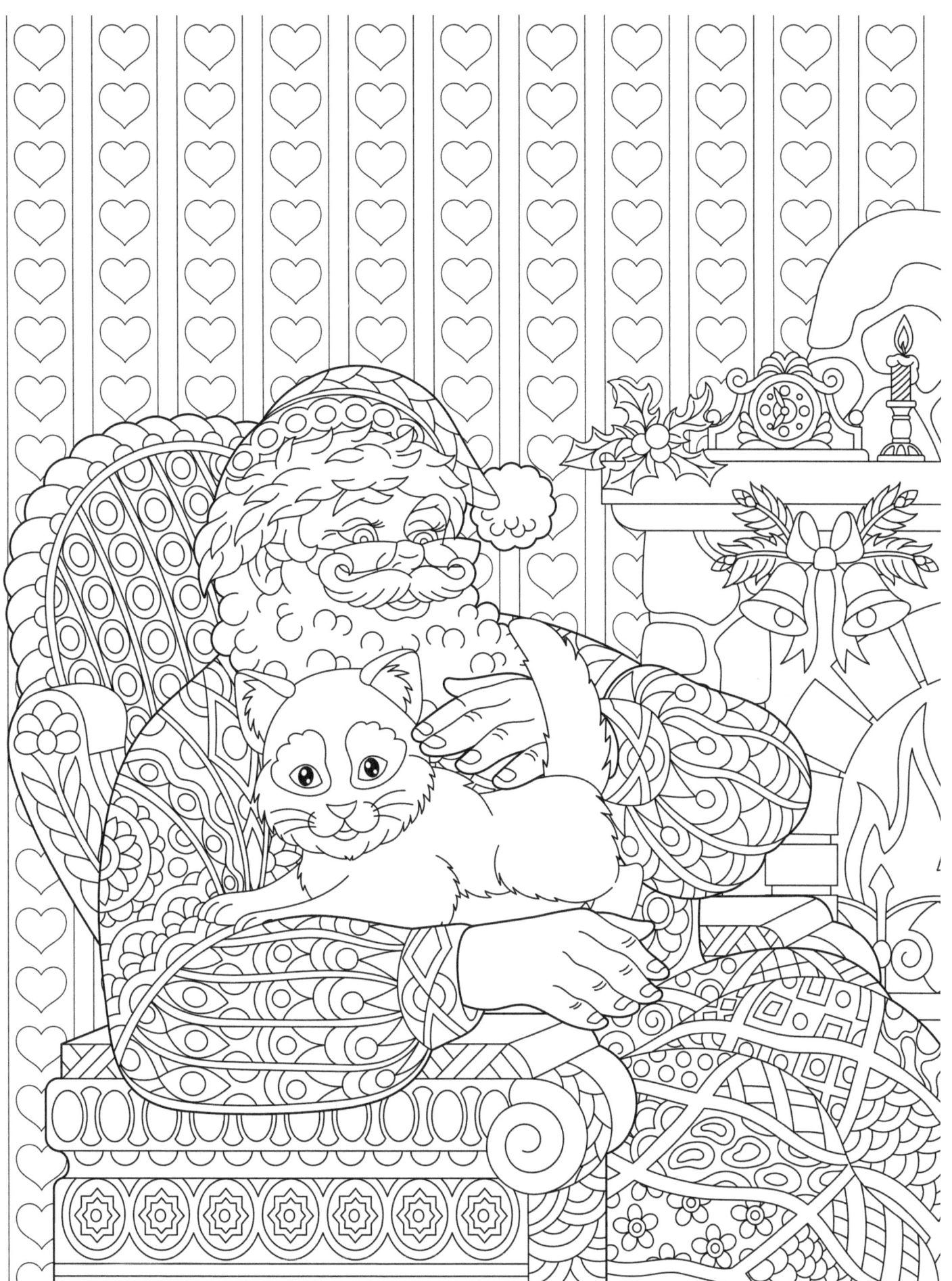

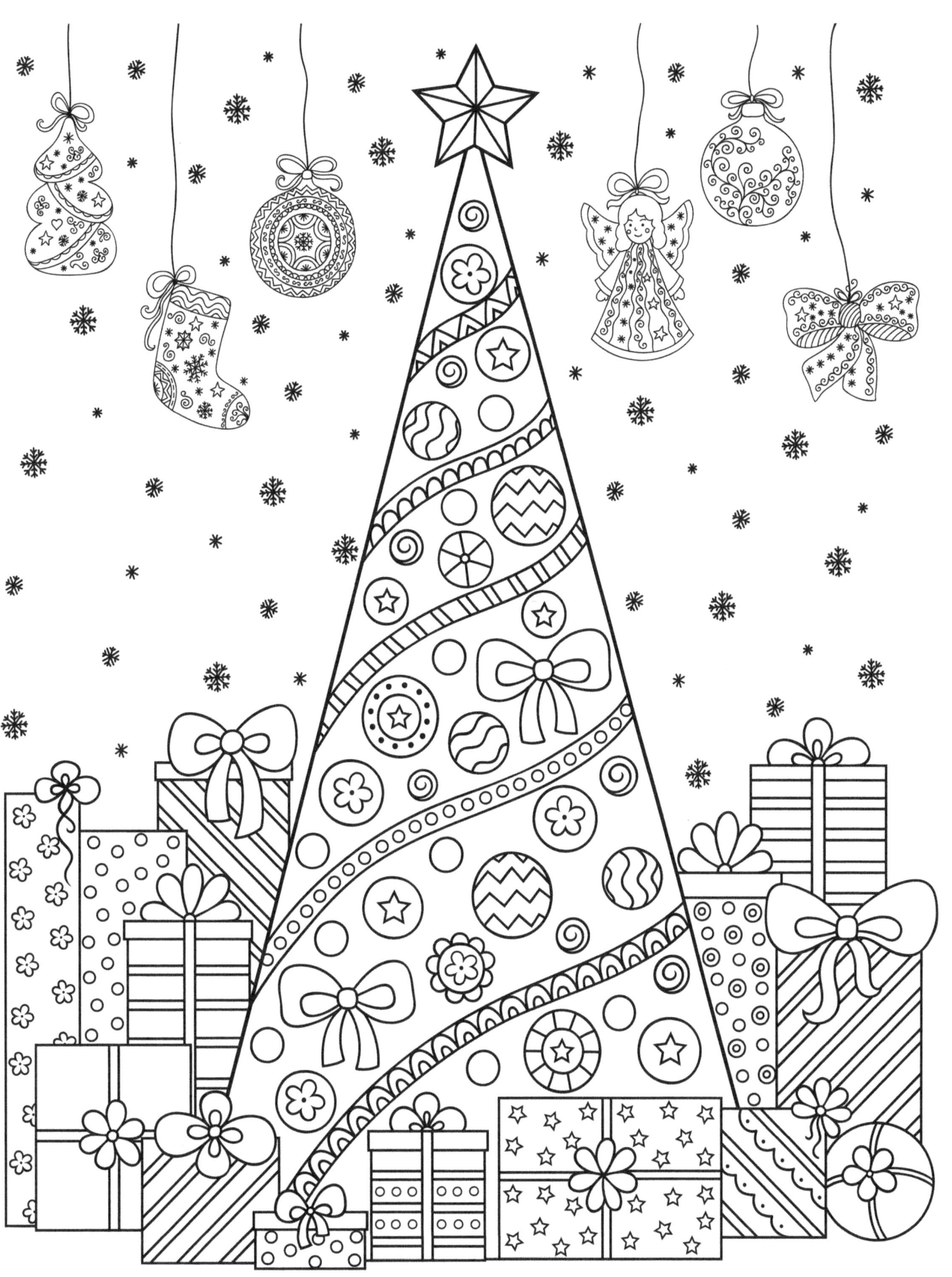

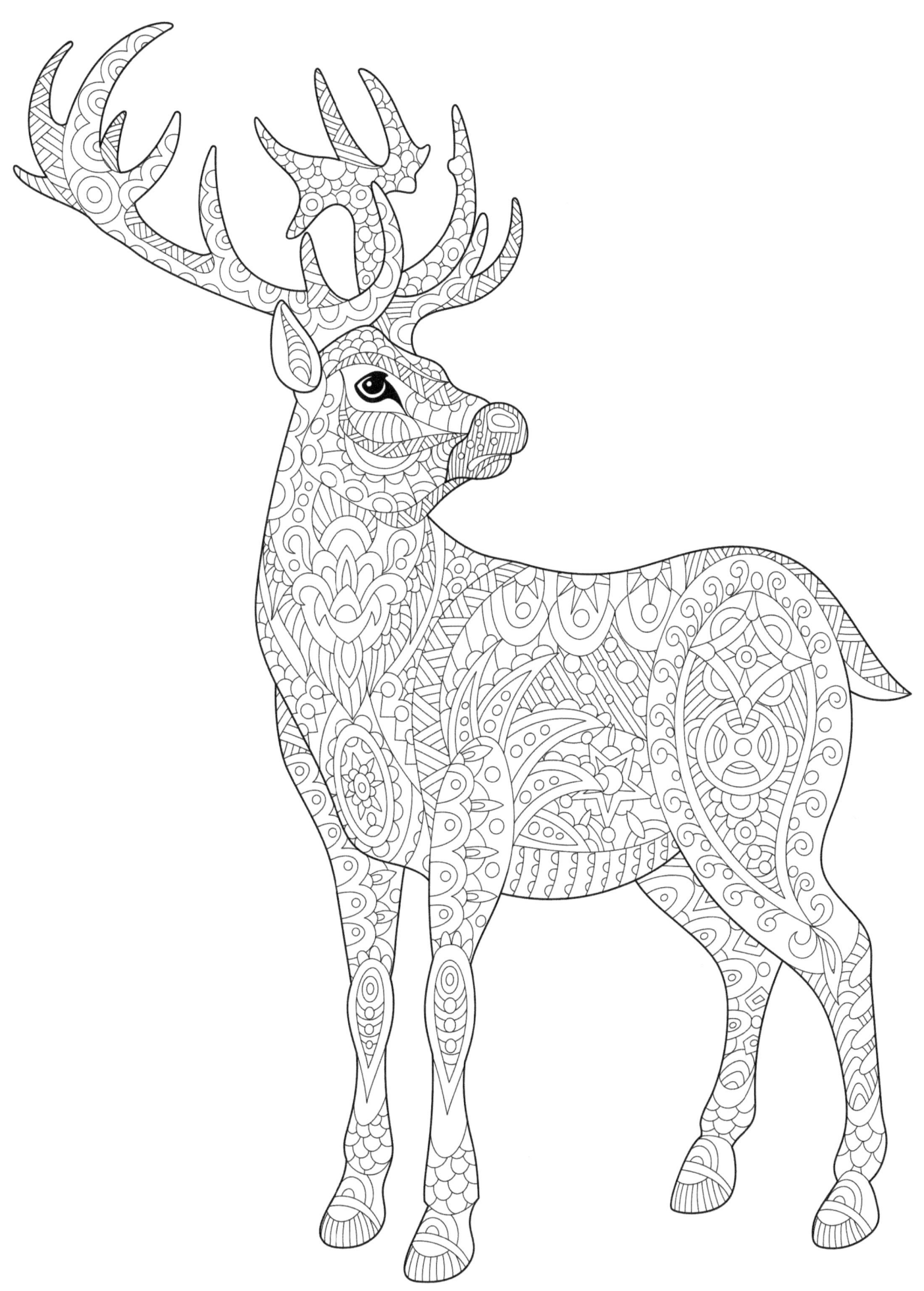

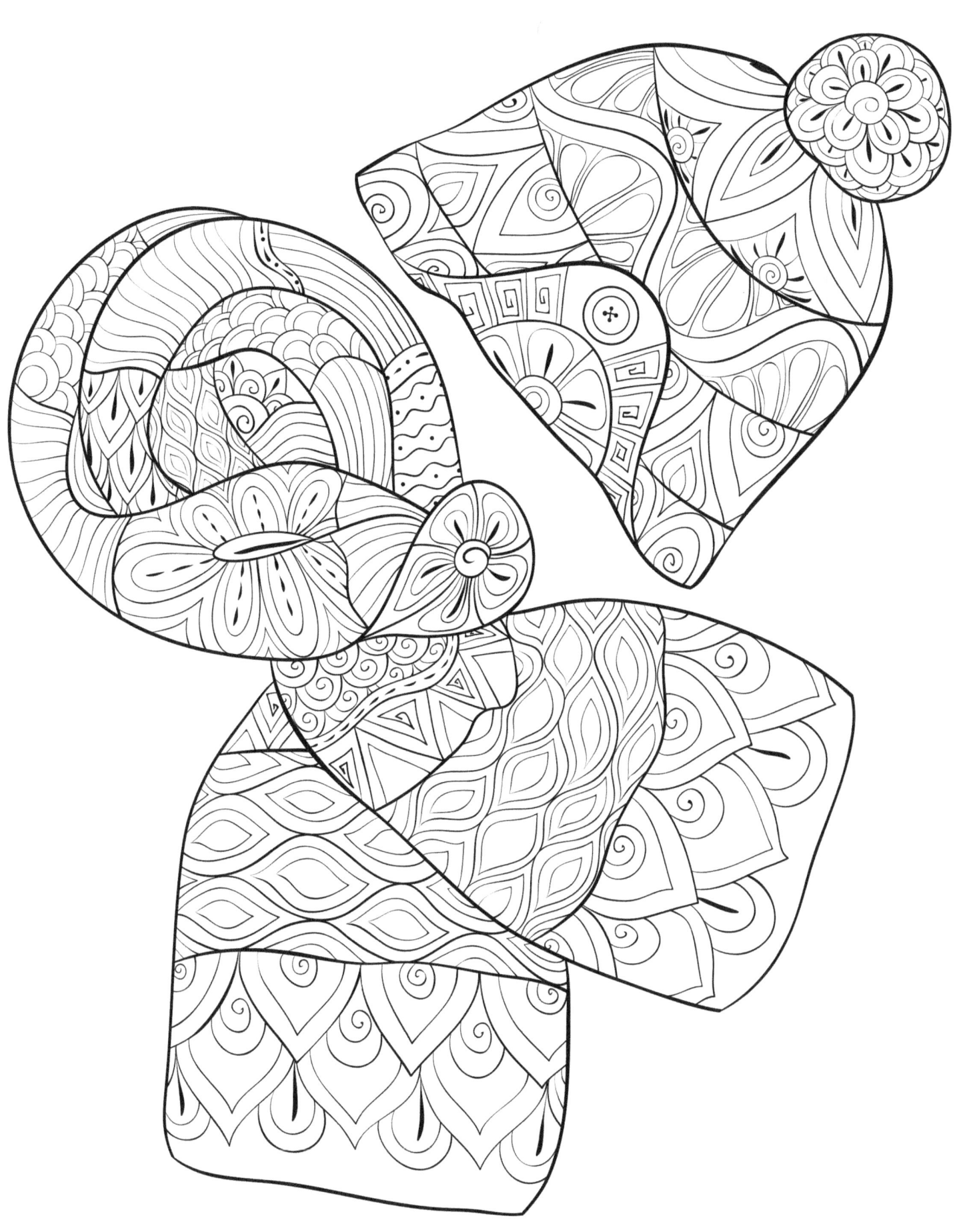

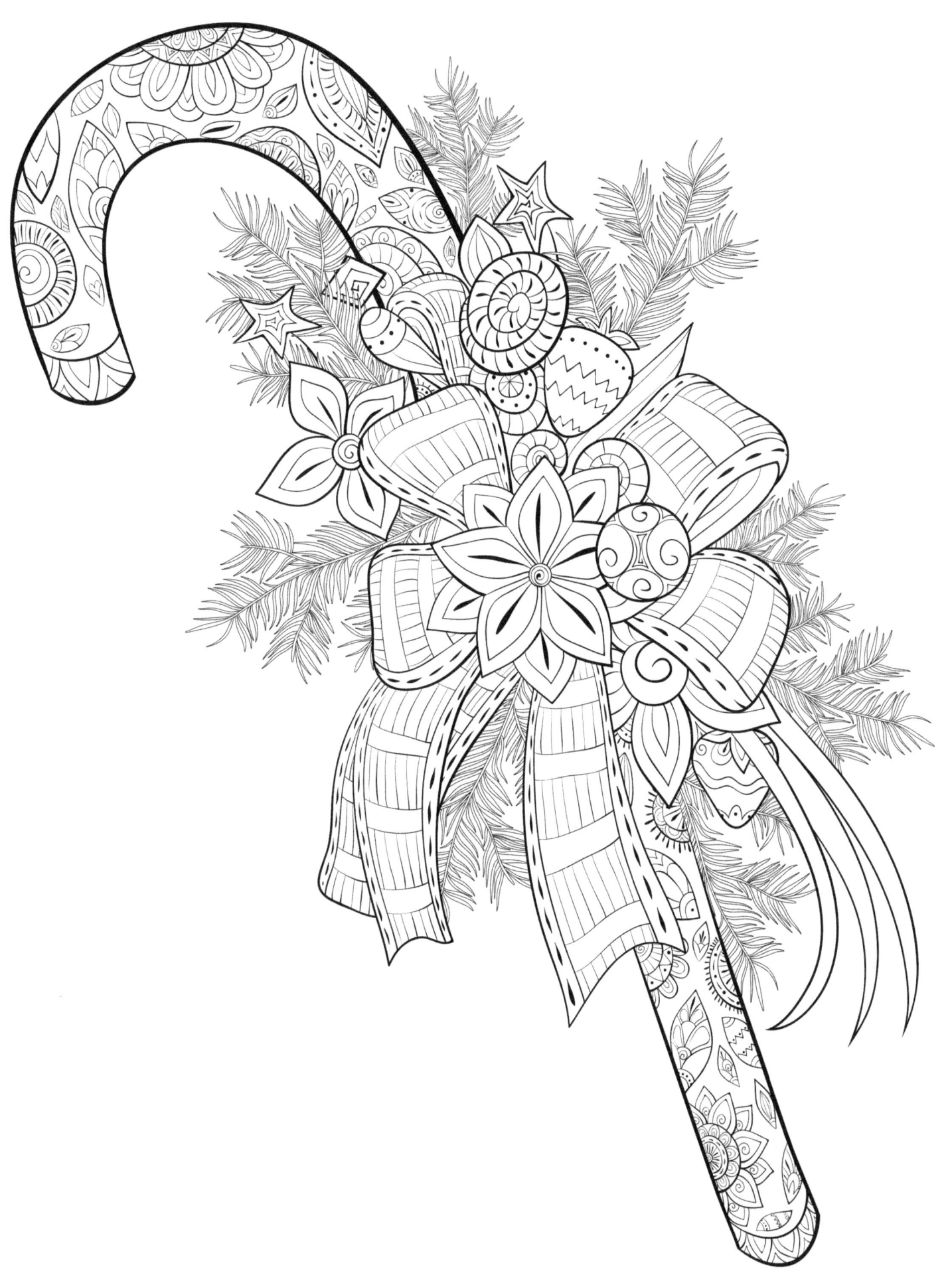

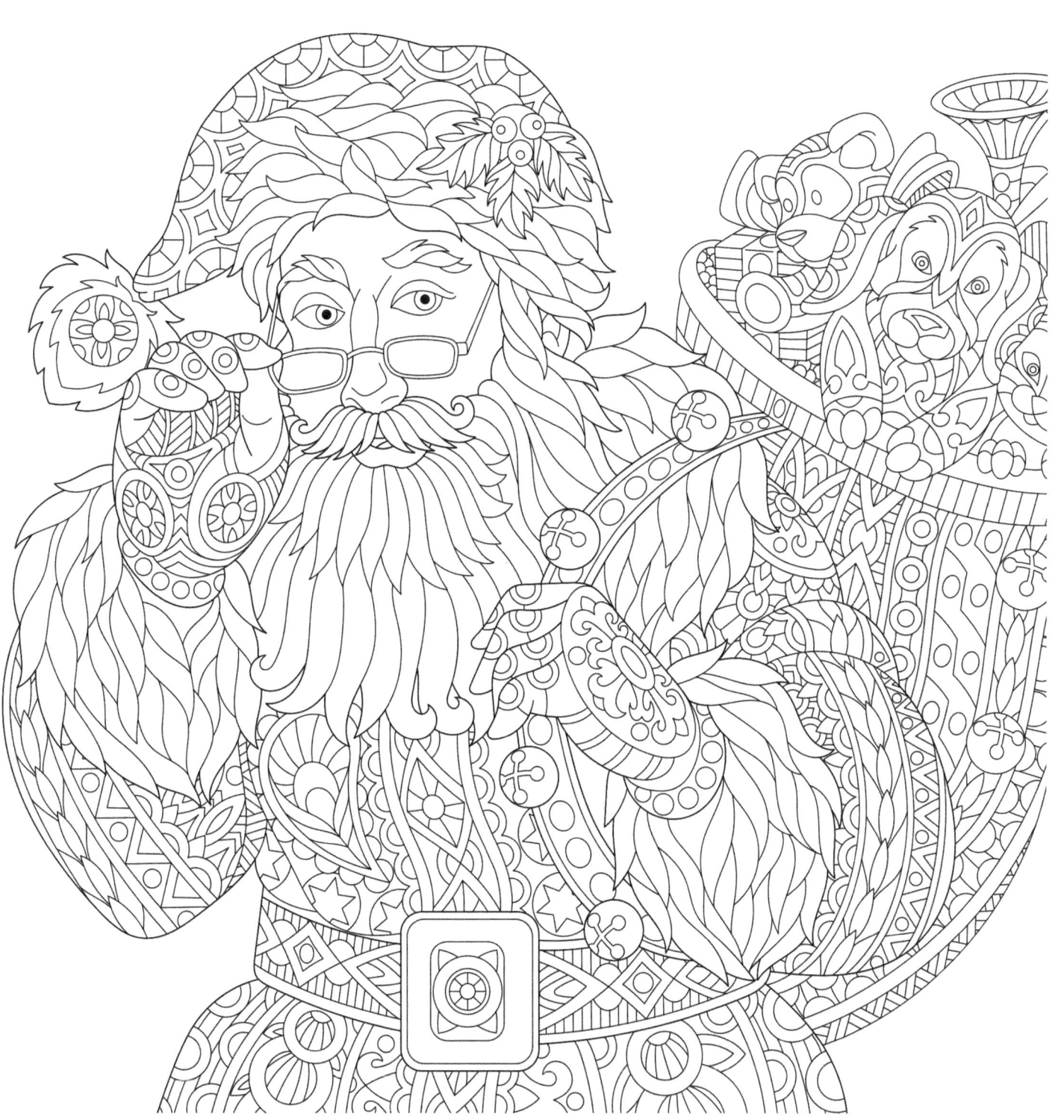

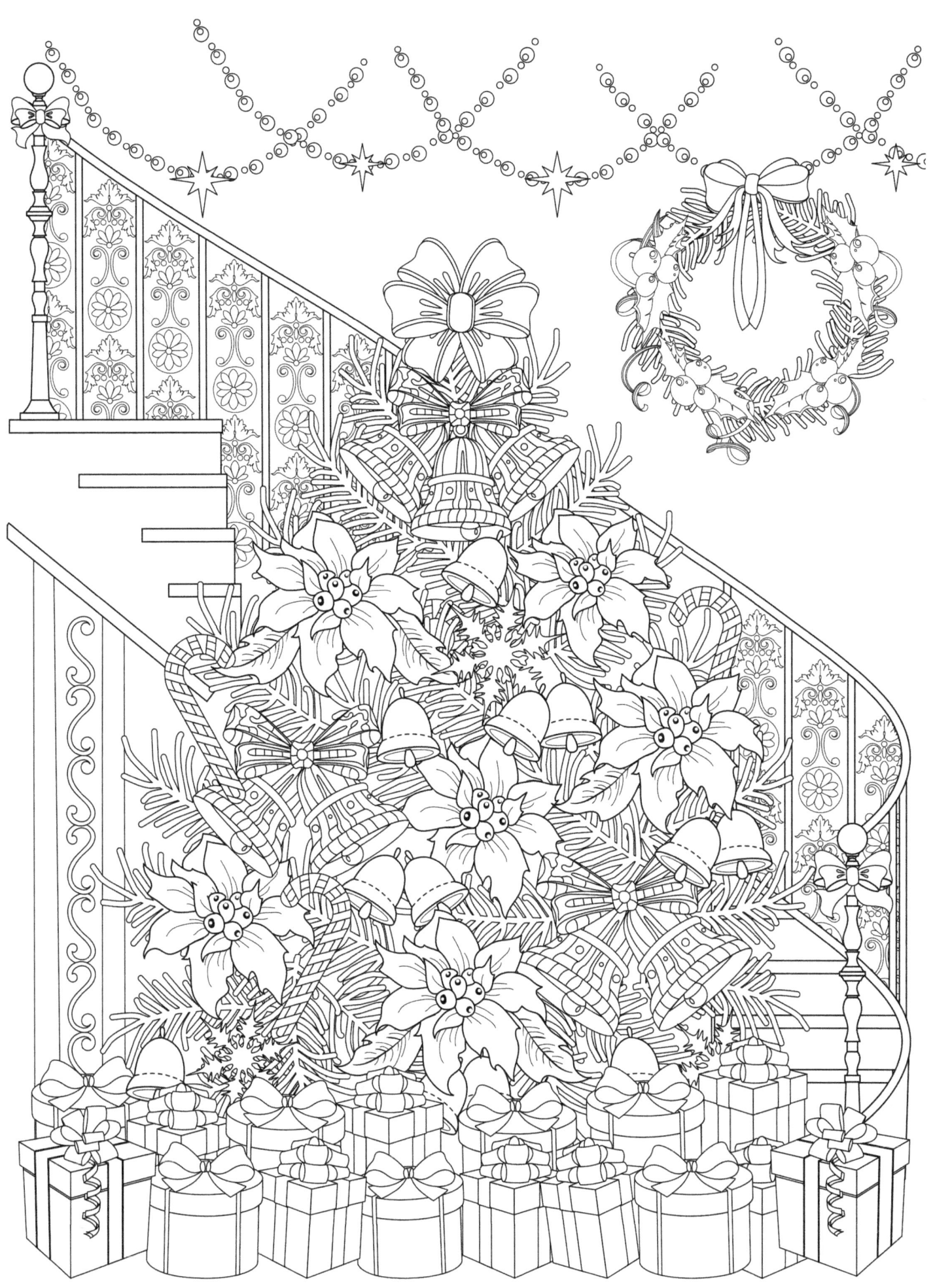

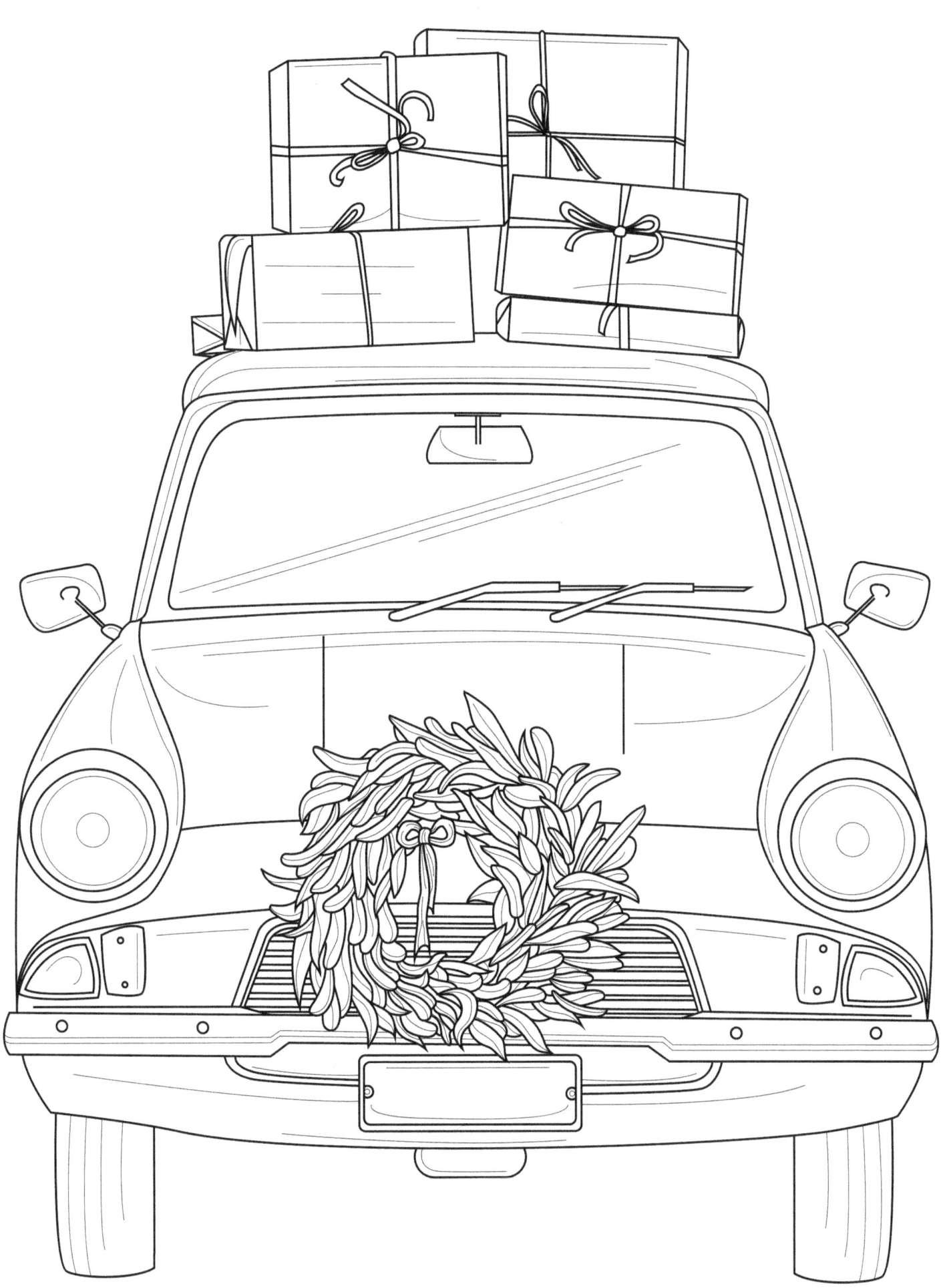

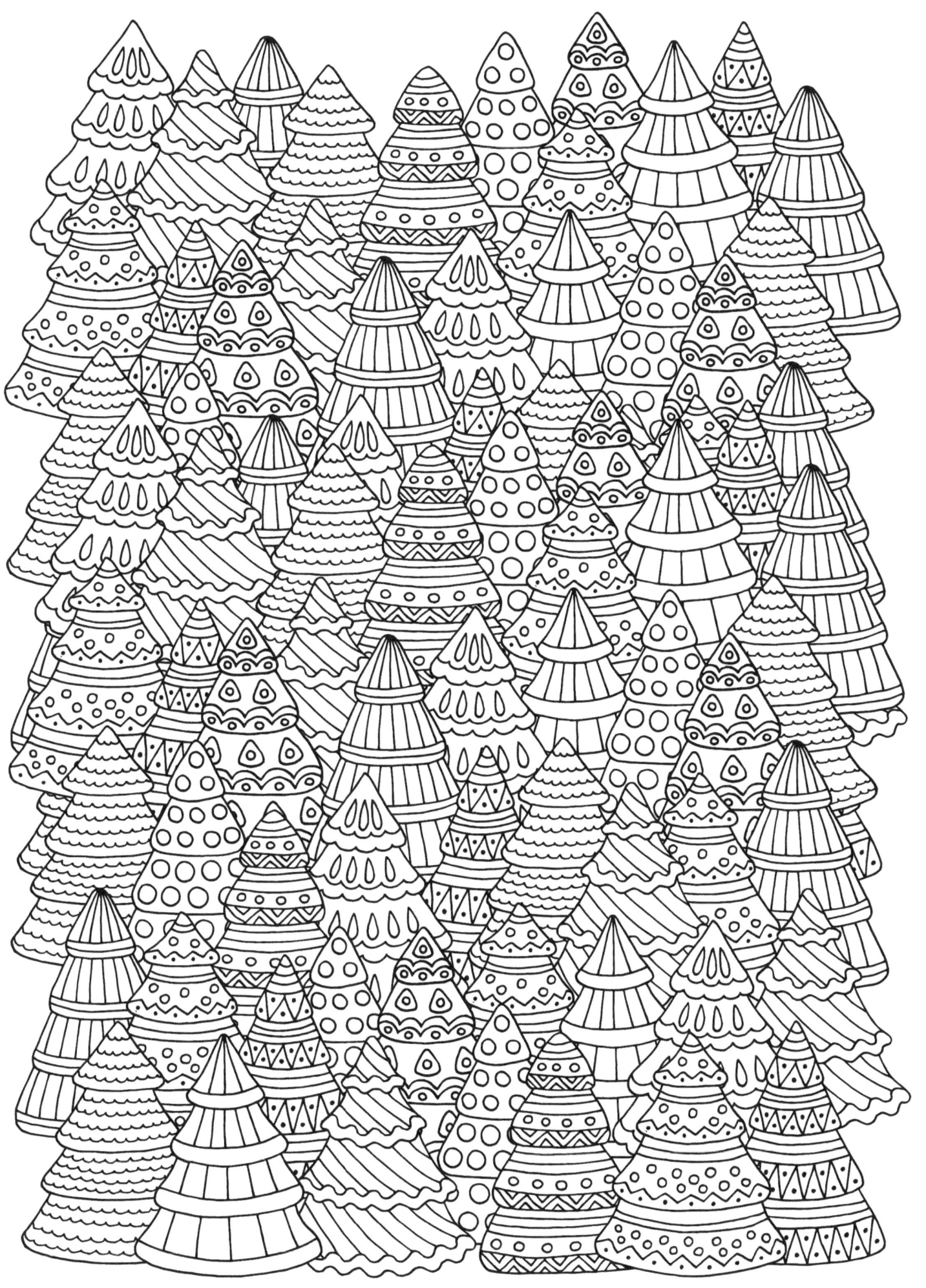

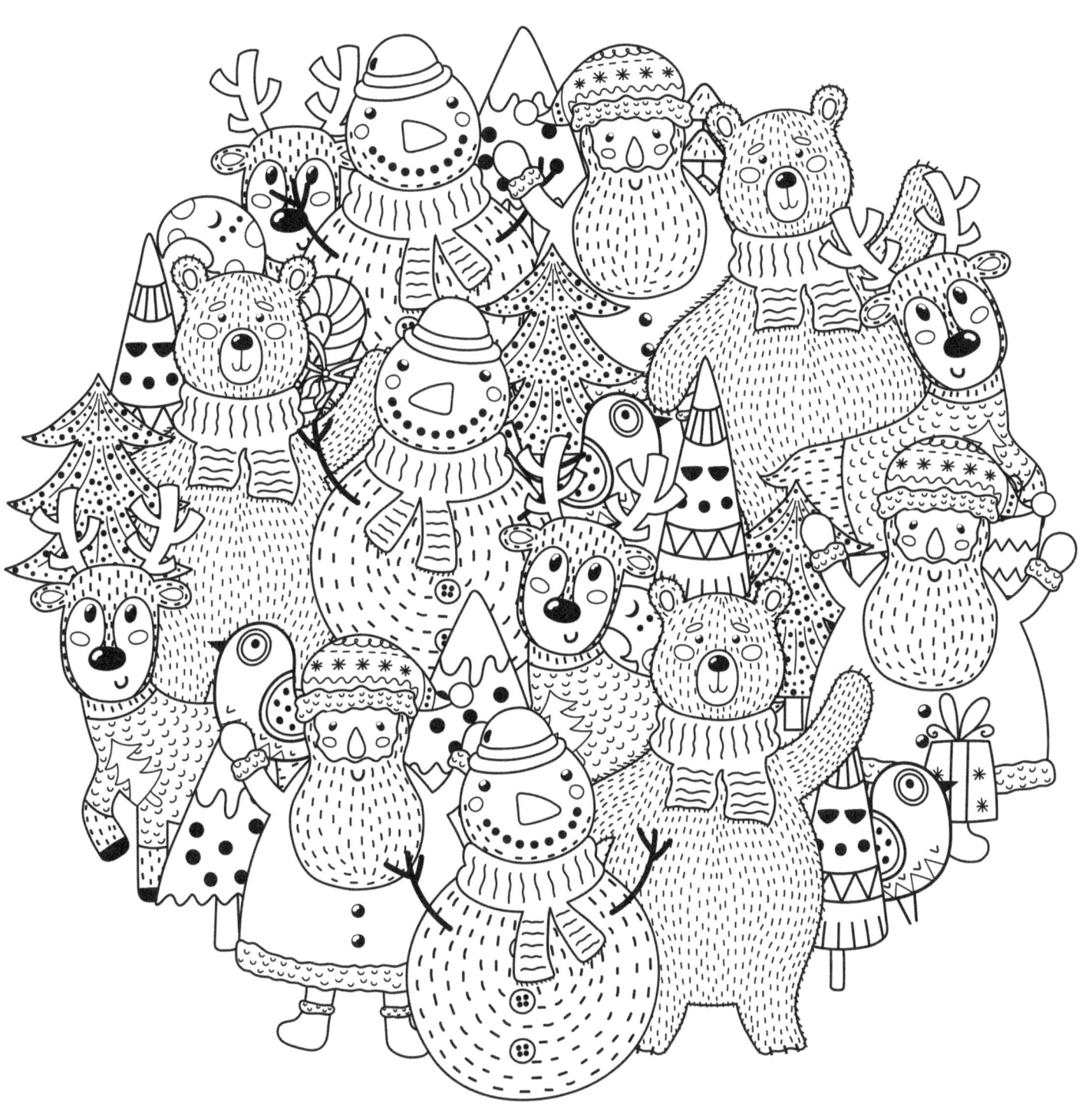

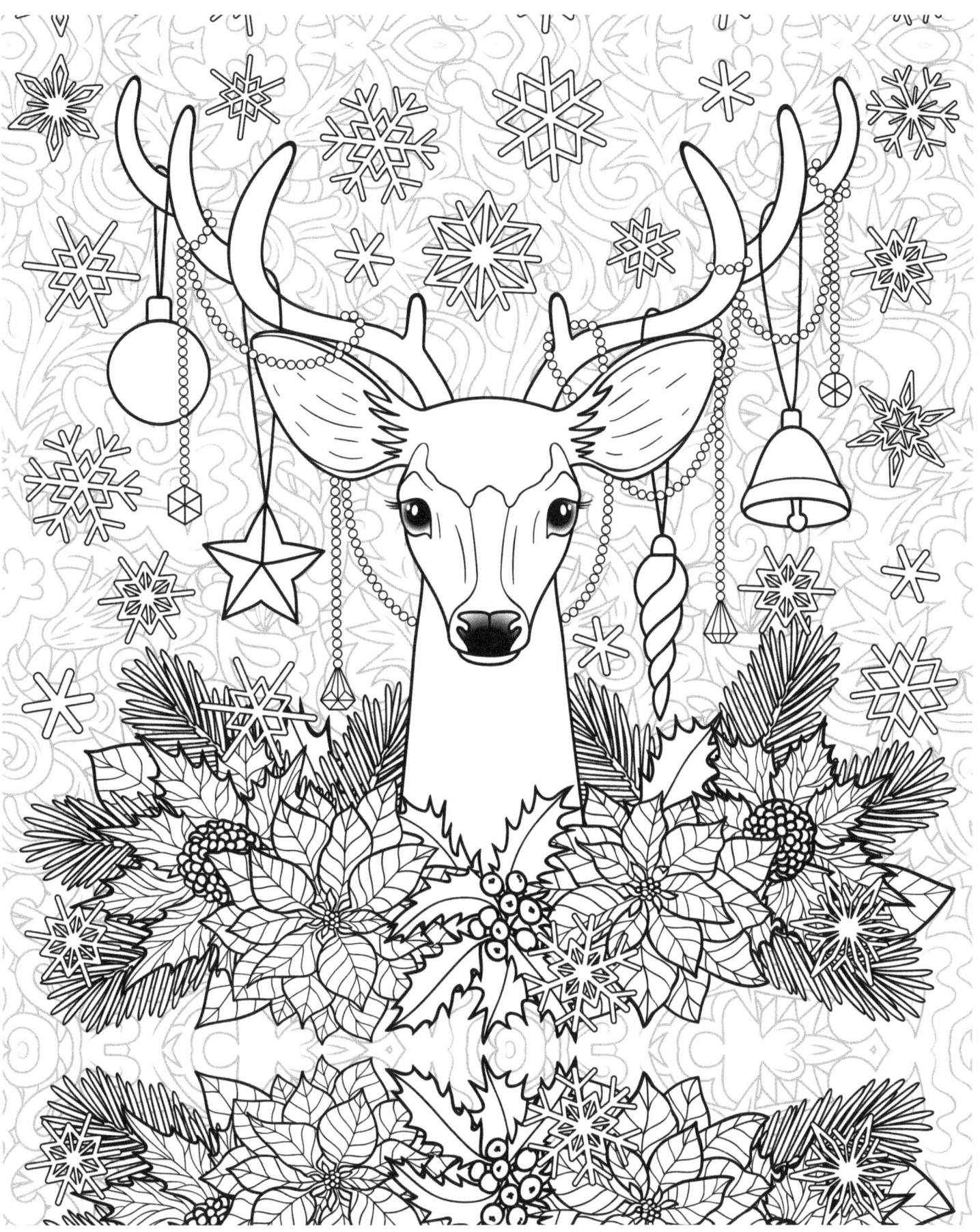

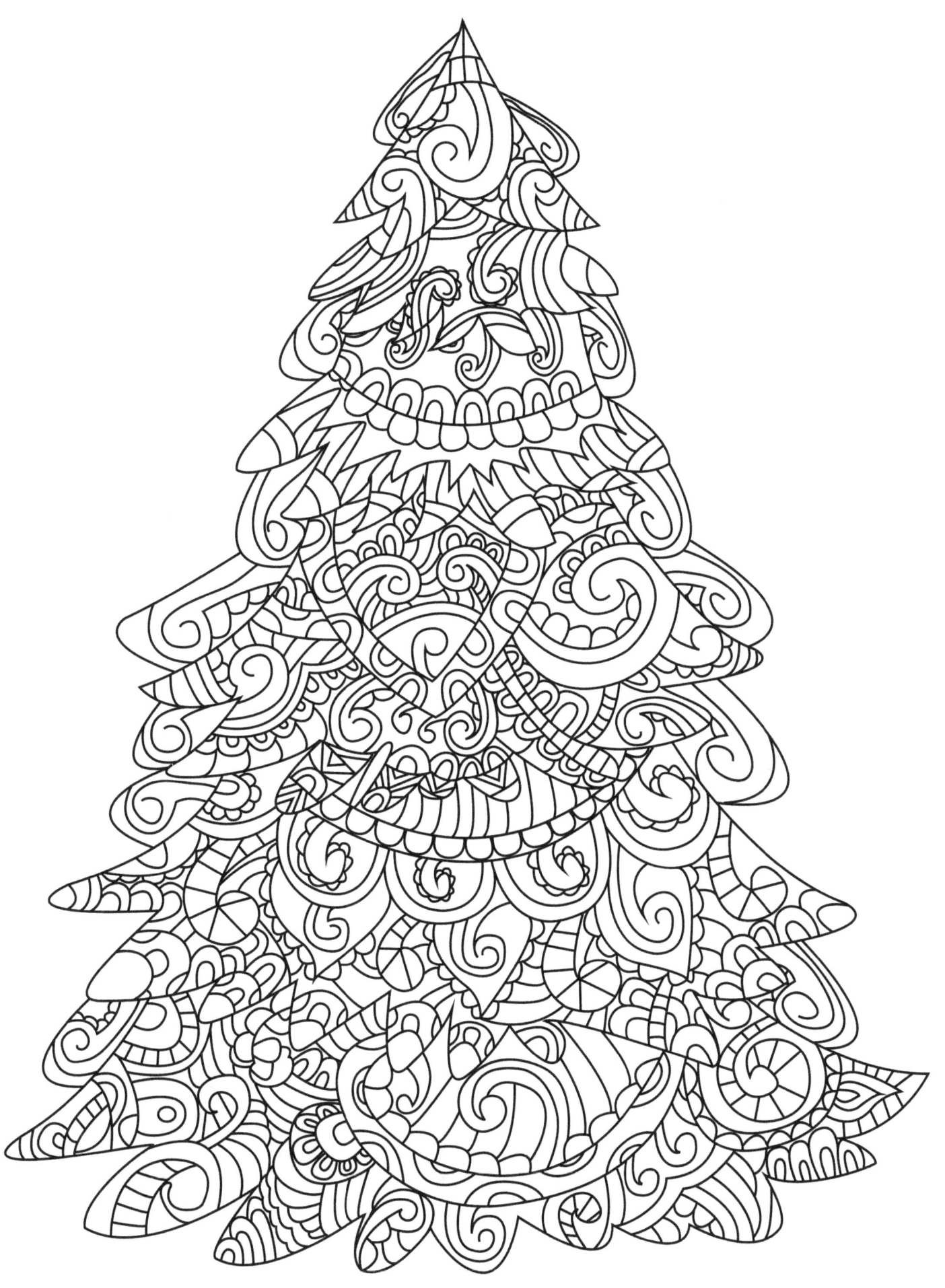

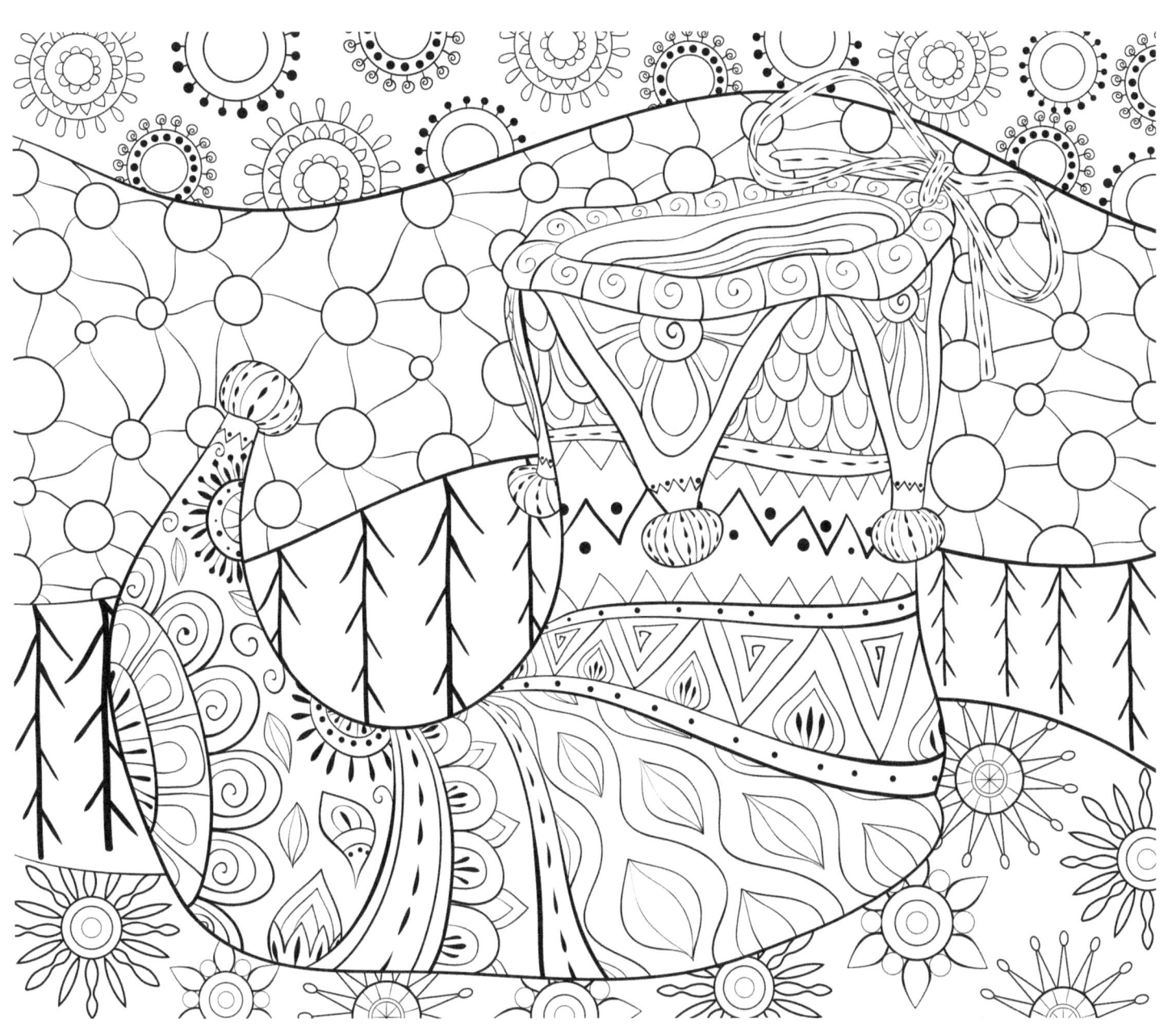

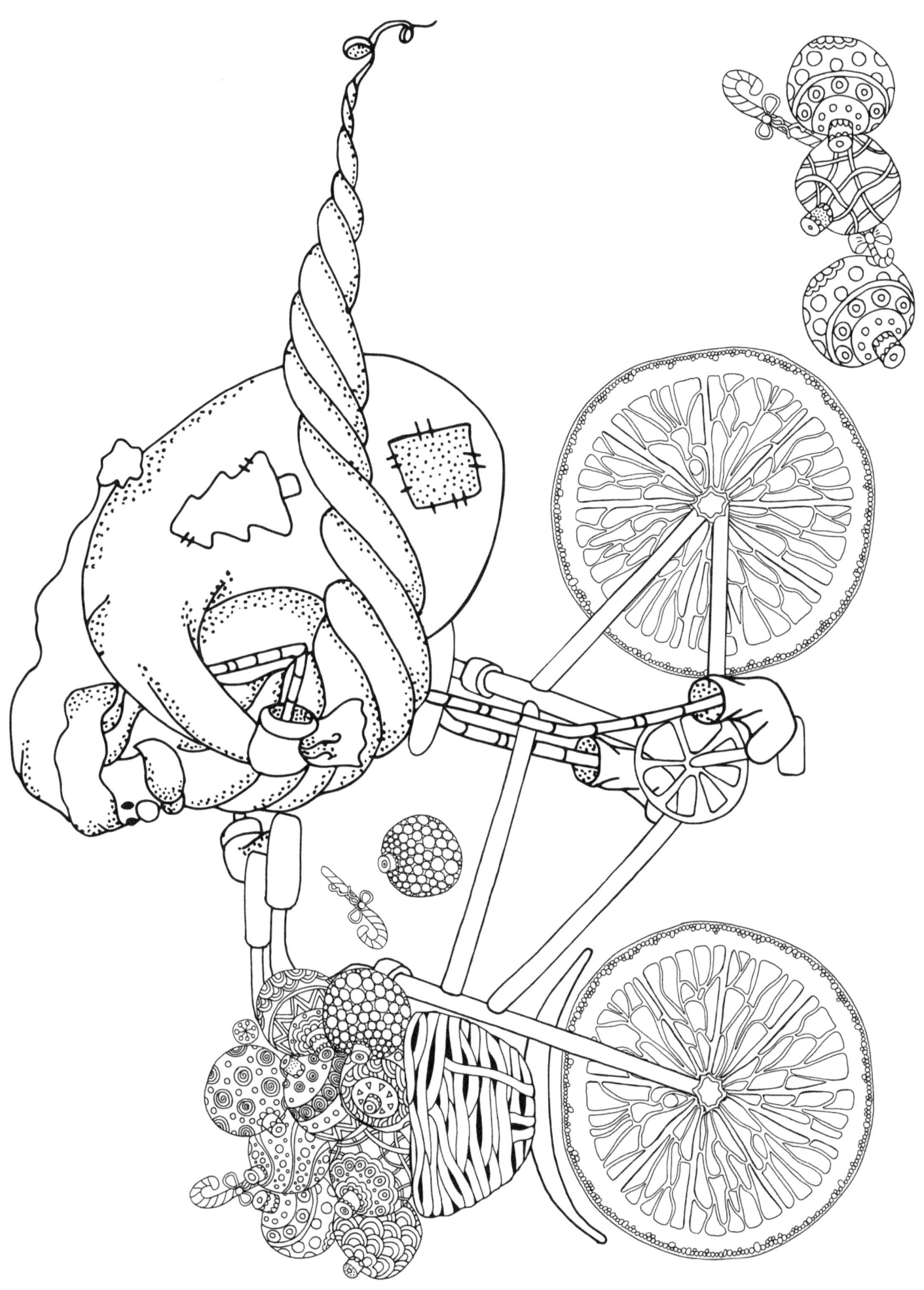

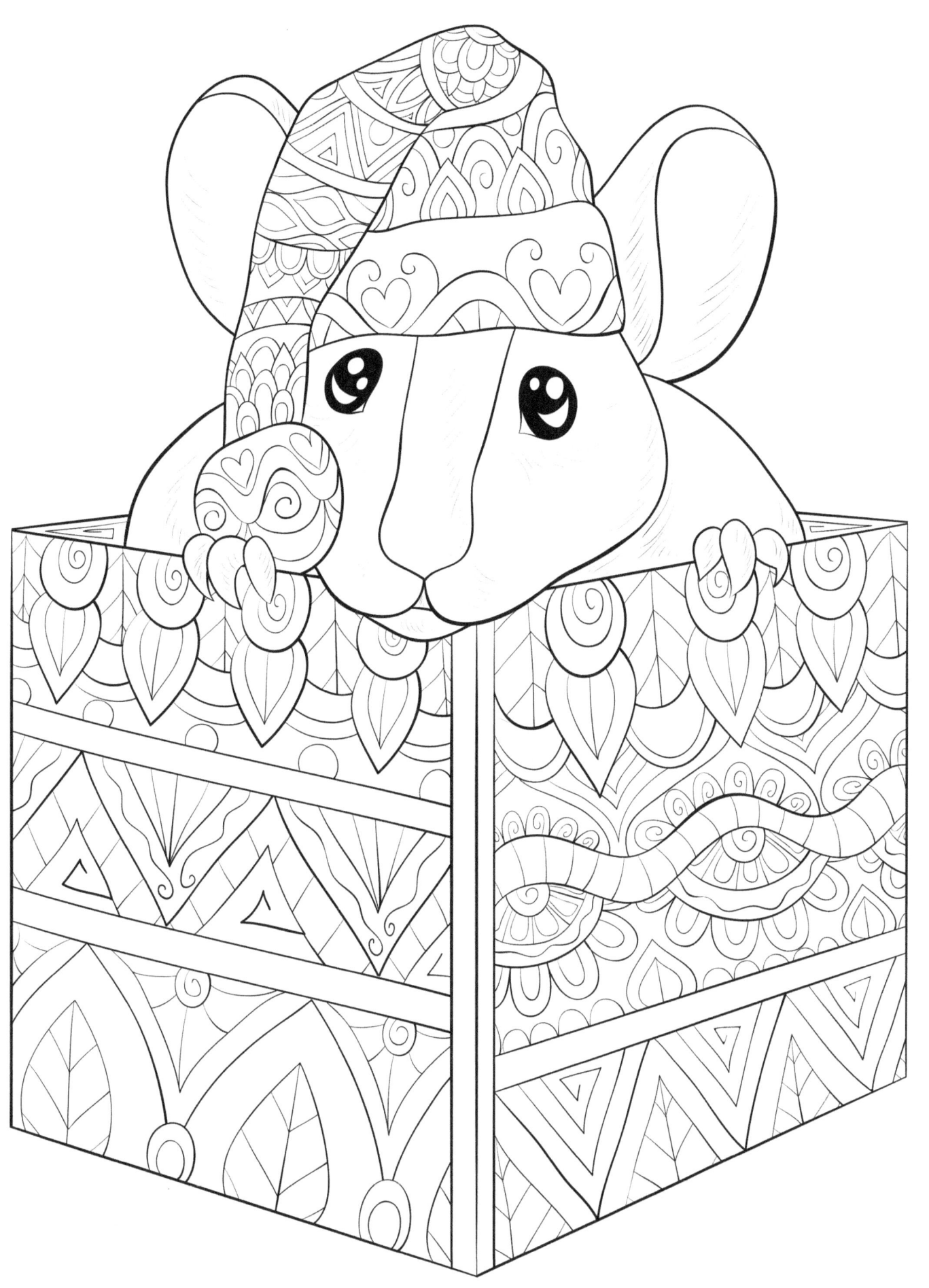

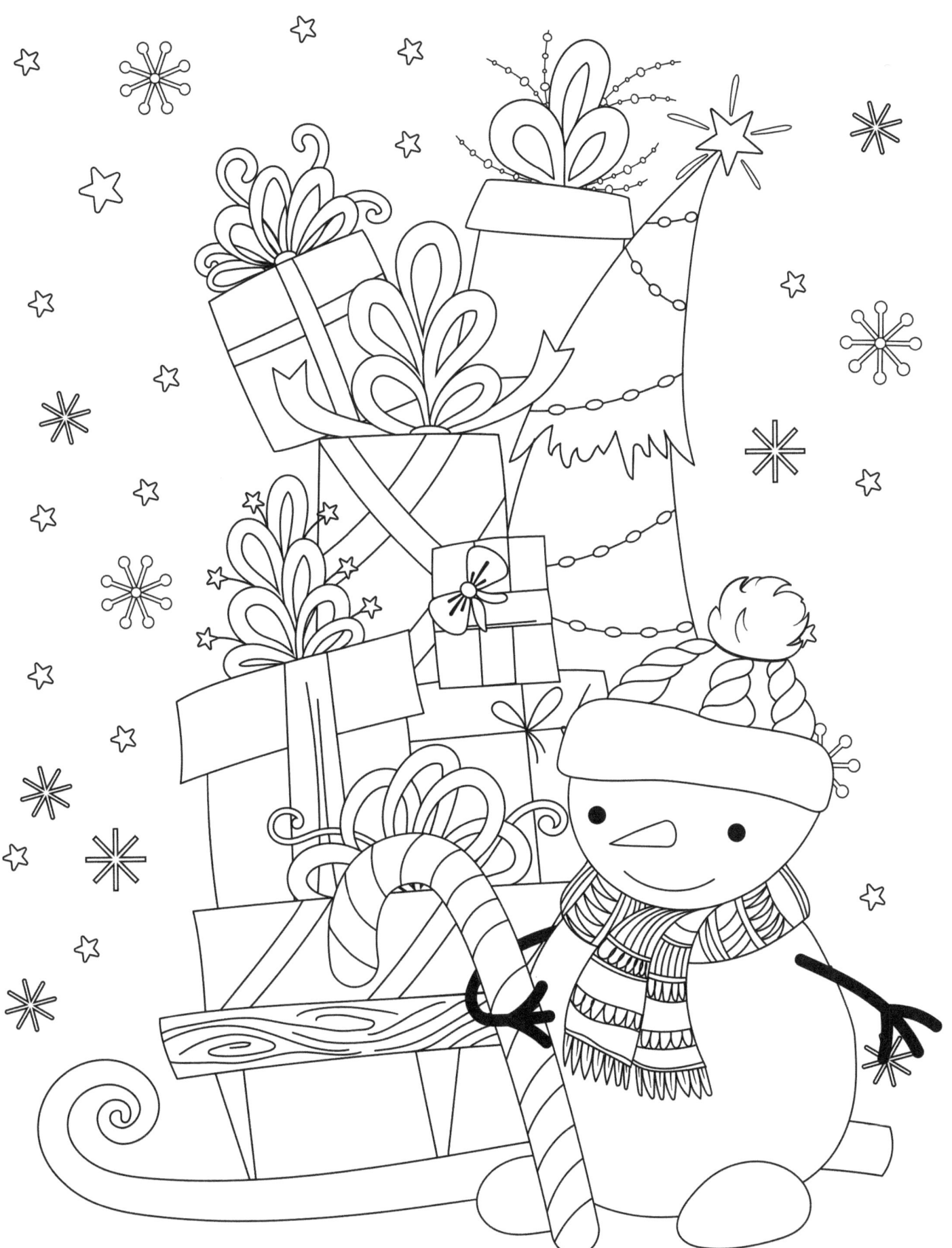

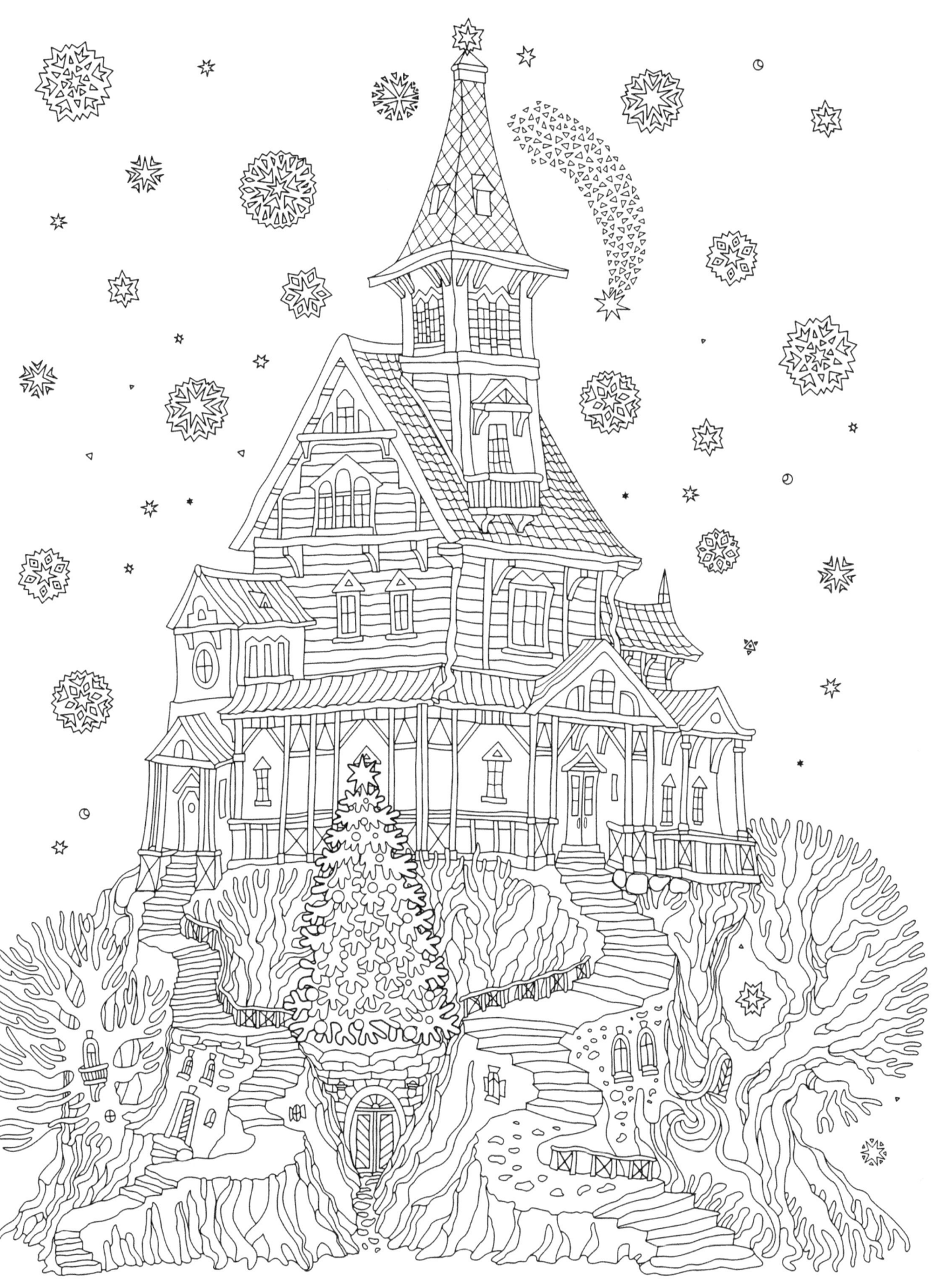

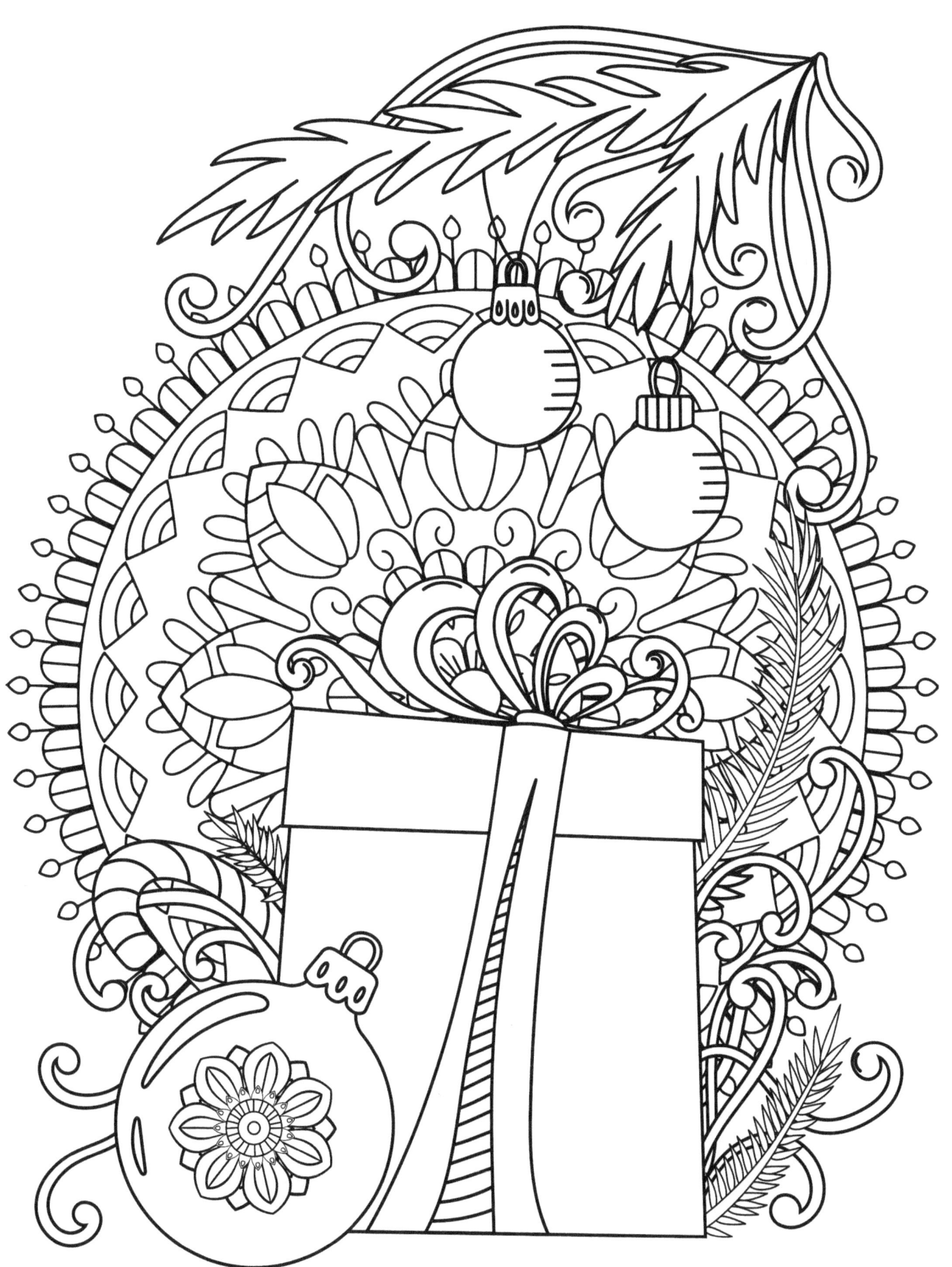

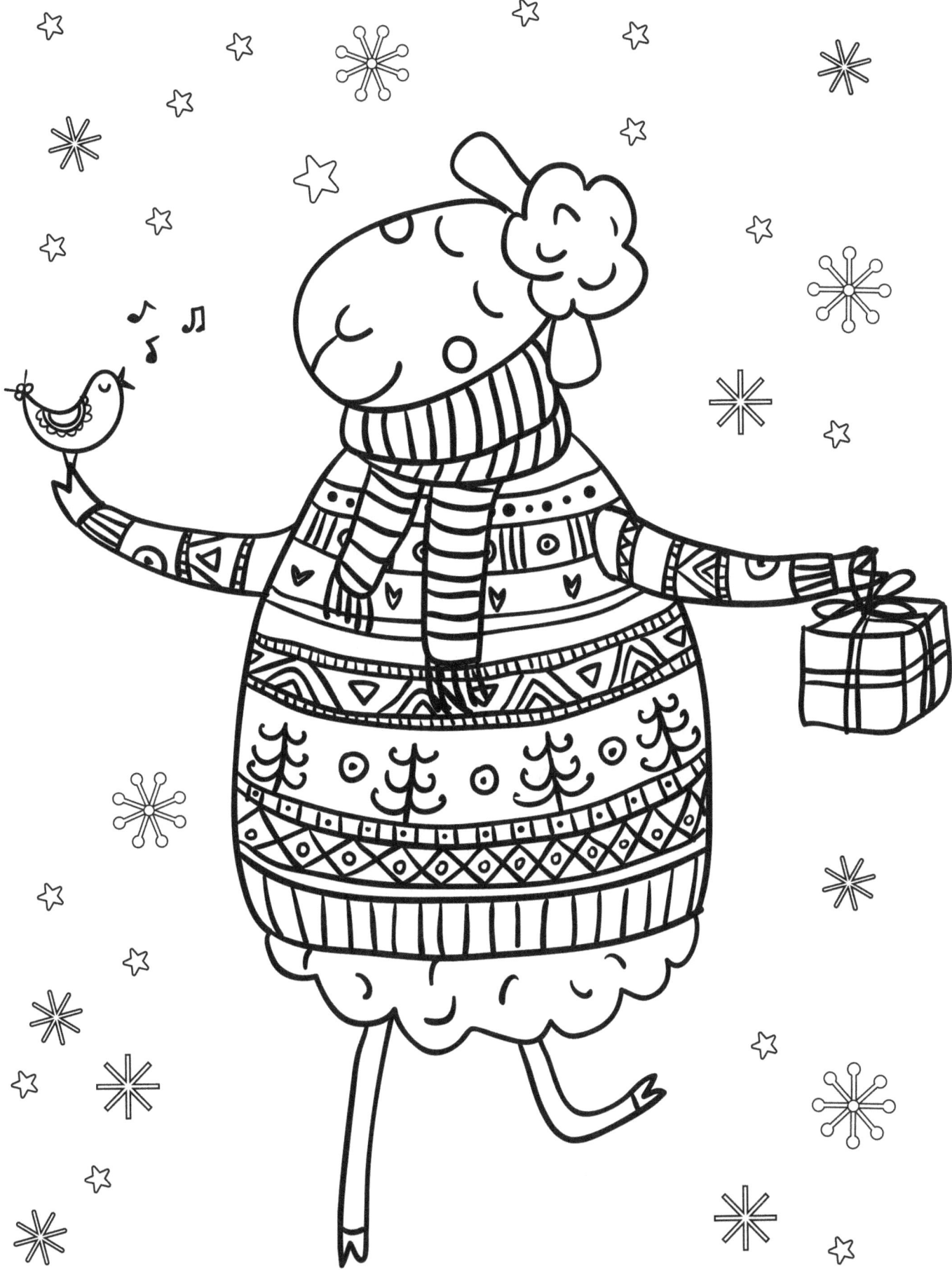

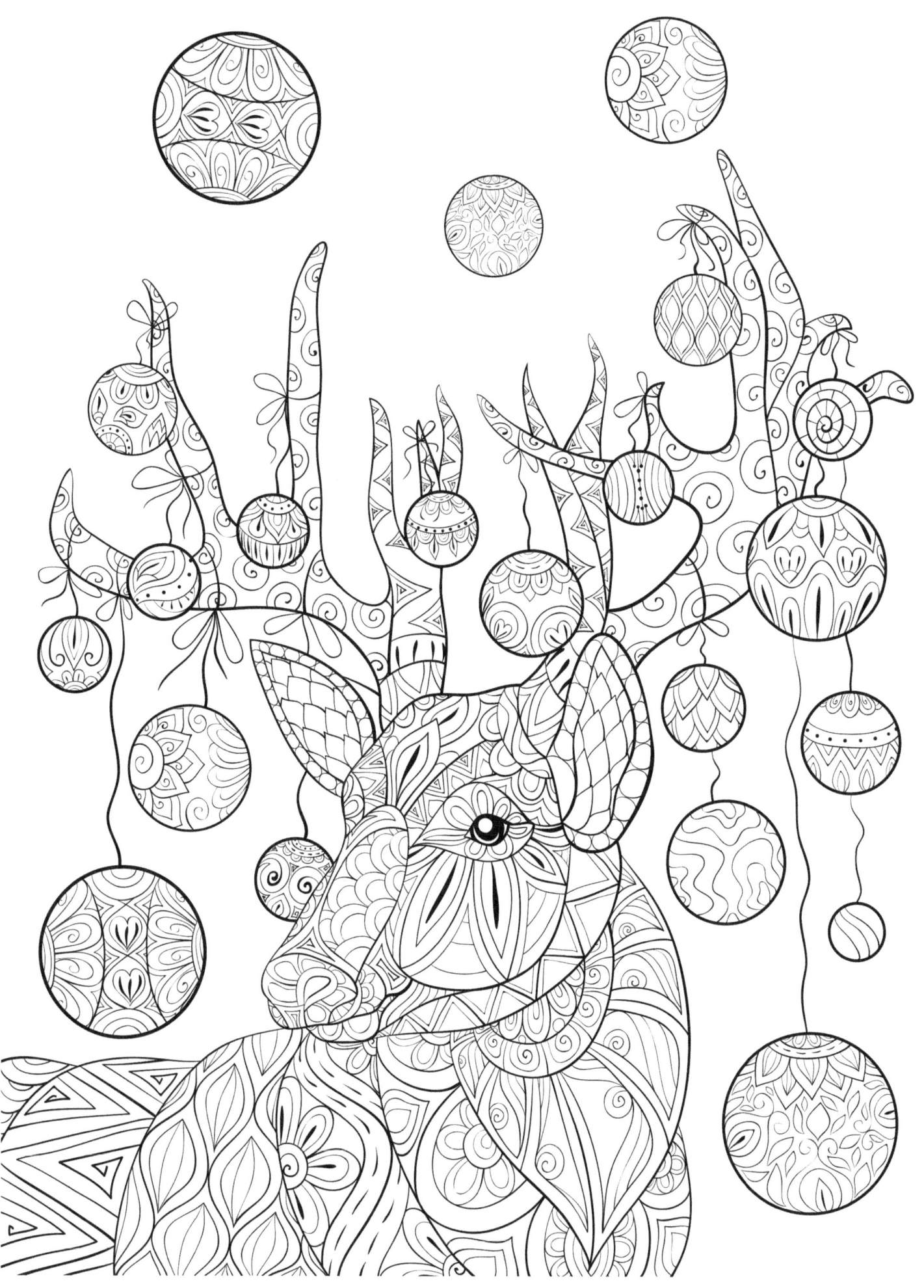

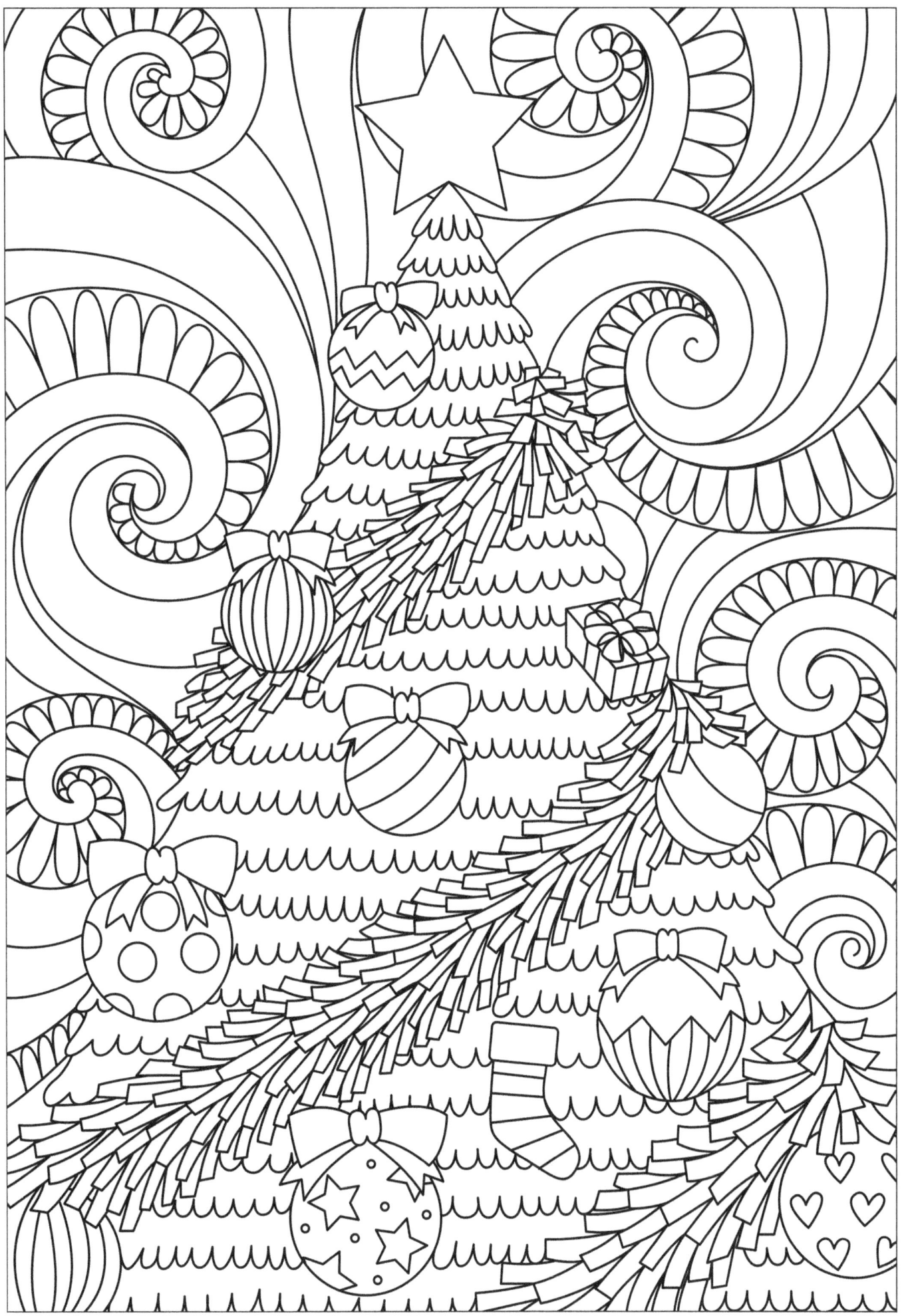

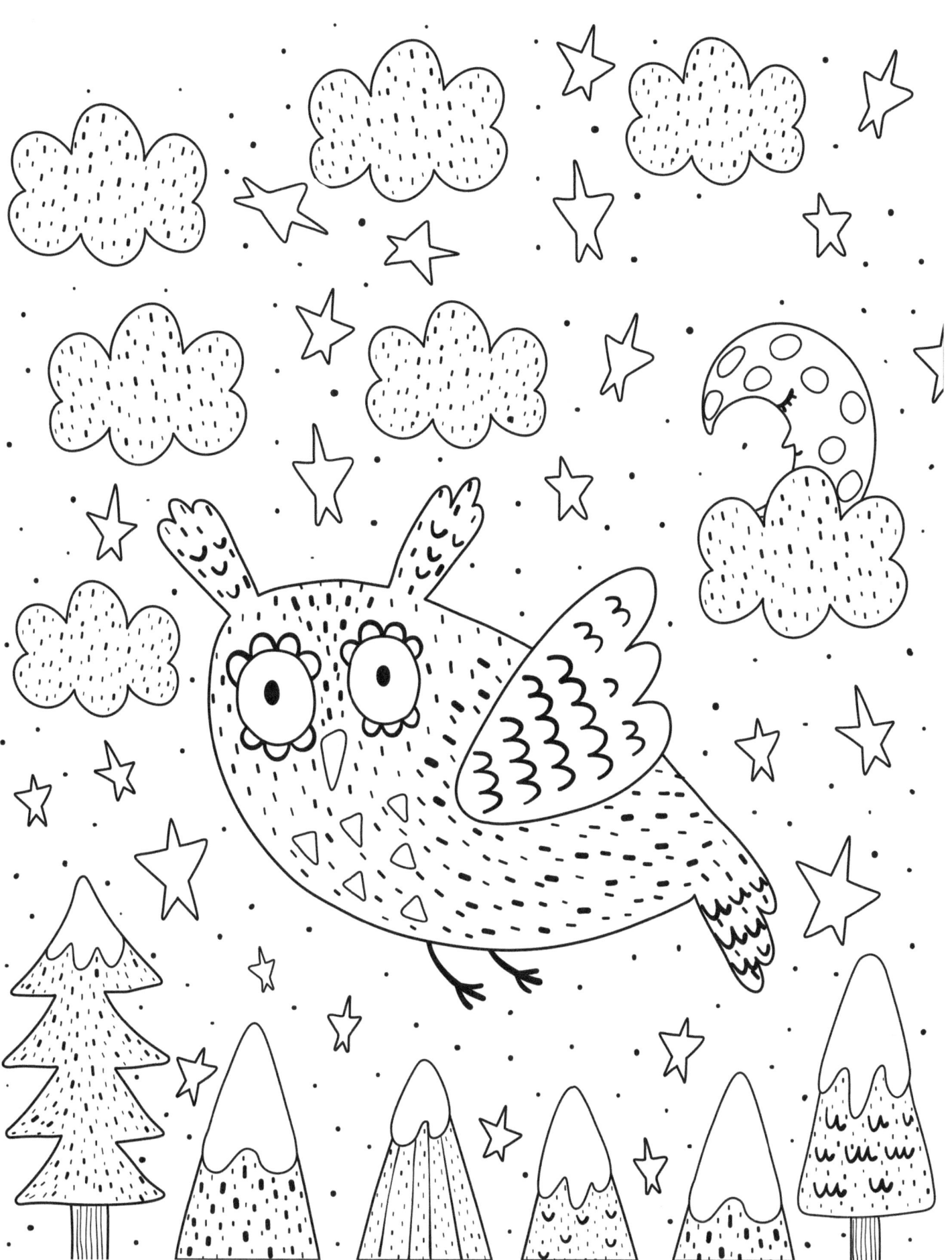

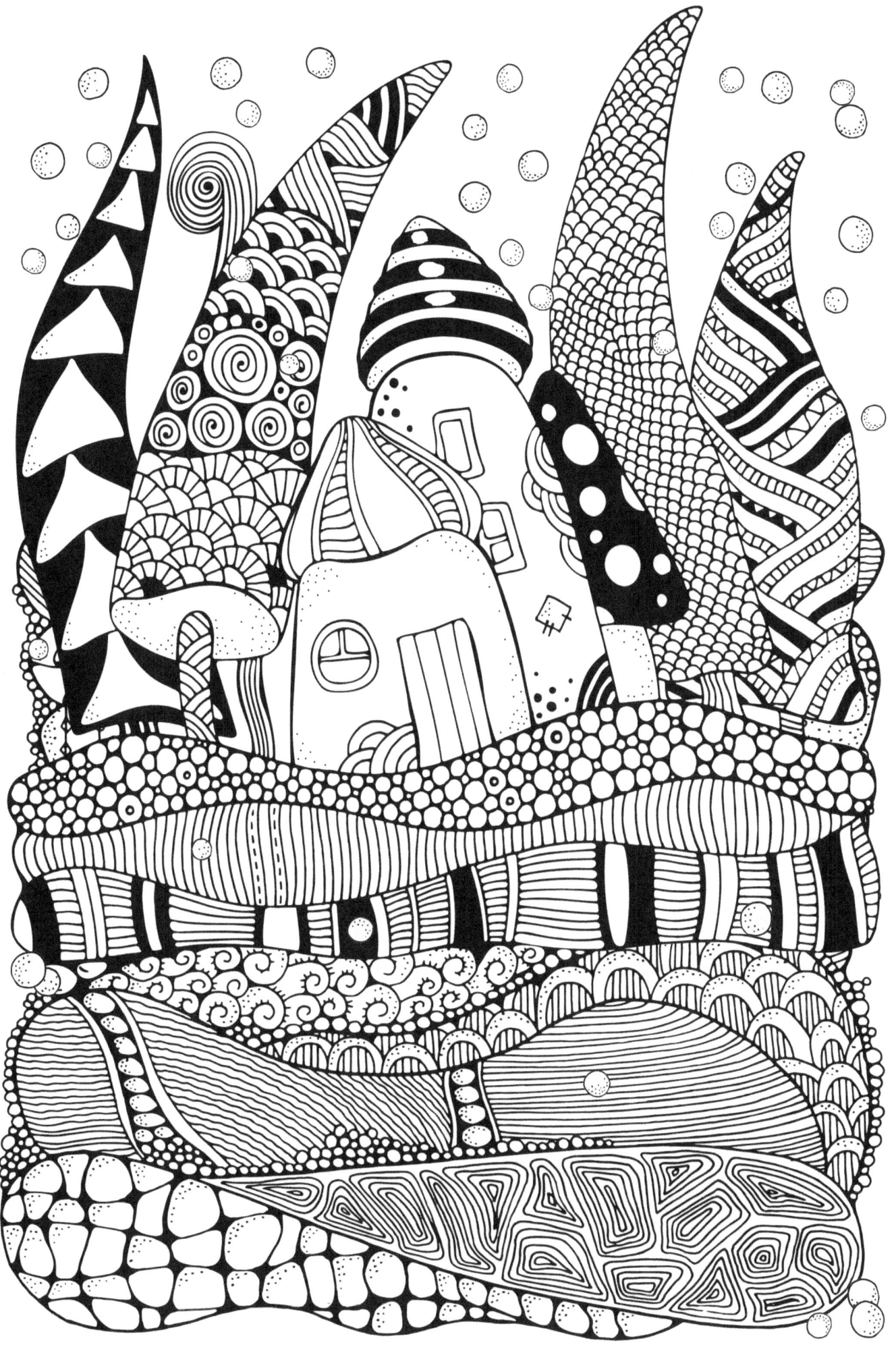

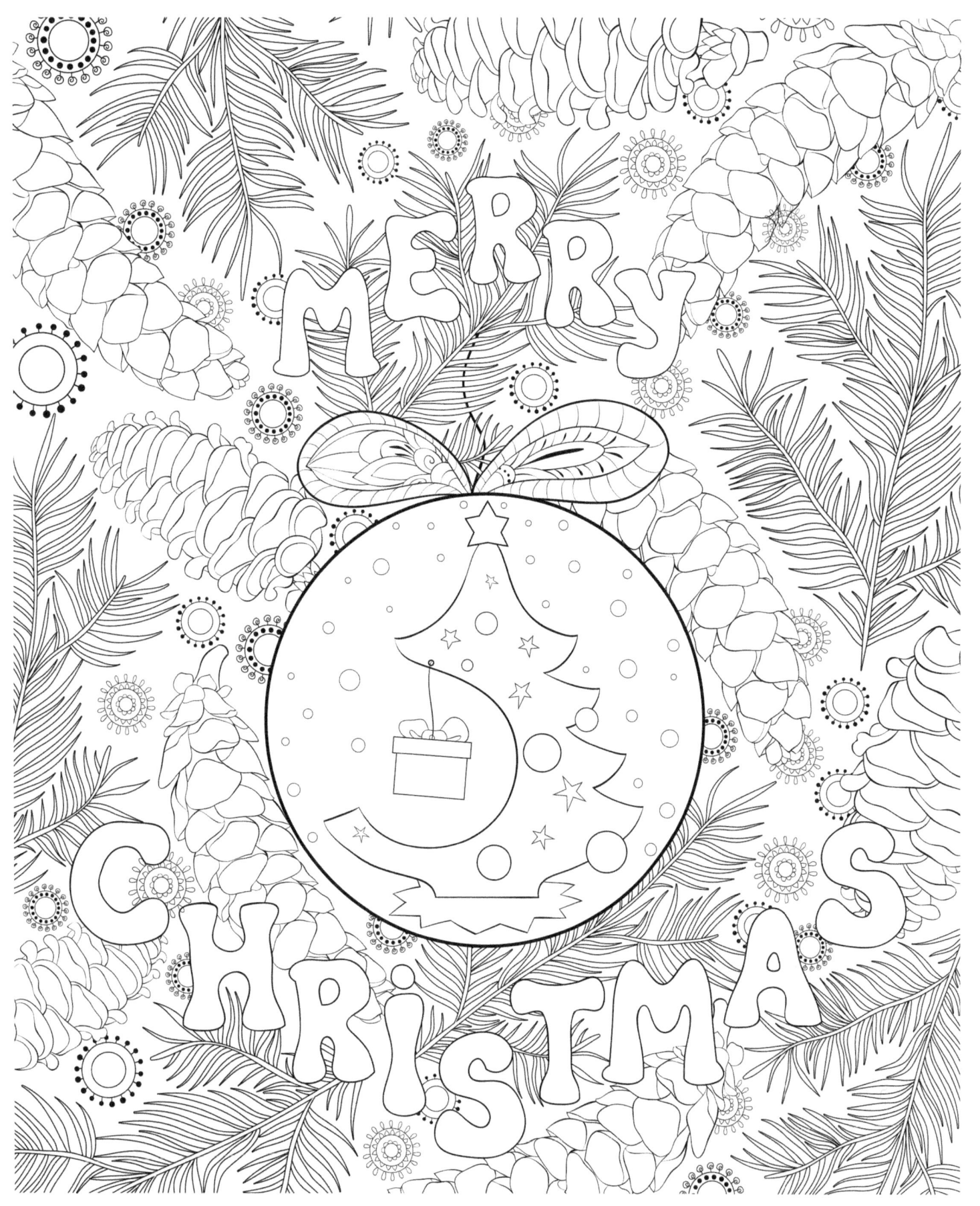

www.ingramcontent.com/pod-product-compliance
Lightning Source LLC
Chambersburg PA
CBHW081442220526
45466CB00008B/2486